Best of the World Recipes

Although these recipes have been adapted to healthier alternatives with reduced oil and no animal products, for optimum health it is recommended that you eliminate salt, oil and sugar (SOS) altogether. You will find pencil notations by me where this elimination is easy:

- Substitute a good homemade vegetable broth for oil (or water when sautéing onions and/or vegetables.)
- Substitute apple sauce for oil in baked goods and pesto sauces.
- Substitute Benson's "Table Tasty" for salt.
- Substitute Date Sugar for sweeteners and sugar.

Two of our favorite San Diego Restaurants are:
- *Purple Mint* - all vegan Vietnamese Bistro

- *Jyoti-Bihanga* – vegan neatloaf sandwich, daily vegan specials, soups and bowls.

- Veggie Grill

Love,

Bonnie

The Best in the World III

HEALTHFUL RECIPES FROM EXCLUSIVE
AND OUT-OF-THE-WAY RESTAURANTS

Edited by

Neal D. Barnard, M.D.

Foreword

Welcome to the third volume of *The Best in the World*, where you will find delicious and healthful recipes from unique restaurants all around the globe.

We'll venture inside the Suan Dok temple courtyard in Mae Taeng, Thailand, to discover a wonderful coconut soup and curry stir-fry. From the Montenegro-Albania border comes an amazingly light tomato soup, and just up the coast in Budva, a tiny seaside restaurant serves up a traditional dish we'll call *pasulj prebranac* (although you might call it baked beans). Or hop aboard a French luxury yacht. Where else would you find a *chausson d'épinards?*

When you're ready, unpack your bags and enjoy the very best restaurants back in the United States. In Ft. Lauderdale, Florida, Sublime's name says it all. From its elegant interior and delightful menu to its extraordinary desserts, Sublime sets the standard for what a restaurant should be. You'll discover its secrets for carrot-ginger soup, tomato carpaccio, and orecchiette with braised vegetables, then finish off your meal with a perfect rice pudding. San Francisco's legendary Millennium and the brand new Seed Café in Venice, California, also share their delicious and unique creations.

Many hands played a part in this new book. Let me send a heartfelt thank-you to all the restaurants who lent their wonderful recipes and to Leah Koeppel for keeping everything organized and on track. Special thanks to Amber Green, R.D., who conducted the nutrient analyses and who, with Michael Keevican, edited the recipes. Thanks also to our able recipe testers Jonathan Balcombe, Ph.D.; Robin Bernstein; Nikki Bollaert; Shawna Broida; Claudia Delman; Tara Failey; Stacey Glaeser; Eric Jonas; Heather Katcher, Ph.D., R.D.; Jacqueline Keller; Carrie Mumah; Judy Nolish; Emily Richard; Bethany

Richmond; and Irena Rindos. Doug Hall masterfully handled the graphics and layout. Isabel Clark and Lynne Crane assisted in copyediting and proofing.

In some cases, we have adjusted recipes in order to substitute, say, soymilk for cow's milk or to reduce the fat content. But each one is true to the original. I hope you enjoy these intriguing recipes from the world's outstanding restaurants.

NEAL D. BARNARD, M.D.

Contents

Appetizers

CURRIED CHICKPEA, SPINACH, AND BUTTERNUT PHYLLO PARCELS

Mildreds, London

MAKES 10 SERVINGS

*S*erving modern cuisine with an international flavor, Mildreds caters to the health-conscious as well as those seeking good, old-fashioned comfort food.

3/4 pound butternut squash
2 tablespoons ~~vegetable oil~~ *broth*
1 small onion, chopped
2 tablespoons ginger, peeled and finely chopped
1 garlic clove, crushed
1 tablespoon curry powder
1/2 cup + 2 teaspoons chutney, divided

1 tablespoon slivered almonds, toasted (optional)
1 tablespoon raisins
1 tablespoon ketchup
1 cup water
1 15-ounce can chickpeas, drained
4 cups spinach, chopped
1 tablespoon fresh cilantro, chopped
5 sheets vegan phyllo dough

Preheat oven to 400°F.

Peel and chop butternut squash into bite-sized pieces, then arrange in a single layer in a medium roasting pan. Place in oven and roast until squash is tender, about 20 minutes. Remove from oven and set aside. Reduce oven temperature to 350°F.

Meanwhile, heat ~~oil~~ broth in a large pan over medium-high heat. Add onion and sauté for 10 minutes. Add ginger, garlic, and curry powder and cook for 5 minutes. Add 2 teaspoons chutney, almonds (if using), raisins, ketchup, and water, reduce heat to low, cover, and cook for 10 minutes. Add chickpeas, spinach, and roasted butternut squash, cook for another 10 minutes, then add cilantro. Remove from heat and set aside.

Unroll phyllo dough, cut in half lengthwise, and cover with a damp dish towel. Place about 1/8 cup filling at one end of dough and fold over forming either a triangle or a rectangle, folding over until pastry forms a parcel. Repeat with remaining filling and phyllo dough, placing completed phyllo triangles on a baking sheet. Bake at 350°F for 20 minutes until golden. Serve with remaining 1/2 cup chutney on the side.

Per serving (1/10 of recipe): 151 calories, 4.1 g fat, 0.6 g saturated fat, 23.5% calories from fat, 0 mg cholesterol • 4.5 g protein, 25.5 g carbohydrate, 7.1 g sugar,3.3 g fiber • 140 mg sodium, 53 mg calcium, 2.1 mg iron, 9.1 mg vitamin C, 1827 mcg beta-carotene, 1.3 mg vitamin E

TORTILLA PIZZA WITH SMOKED TOFU

Horizons, Philadelphia, Pennsylvania

MAKES 2 PIZZAS (4 TO 6 SERVINGS)

*A*n essential stop in Philadelphia, Horizons offers this dish as a starter (and don't forget to finish with Horizons' tasty peanut butter bomb for dessert.)

2 10-inch or 12-inch whole-wheat flour tortillas	1/4 cup red onion, chopped
1 cup shredded vegan cheese or vegan sour cream	2 tablespoons capers
	2 tablespoons black olives, chopped
12 ounces smoked tofu, chopped	2 tablespoons fresh dill, chopped
	2 small plum tomatoes, chopped

Preheat oven to 400°F.

Place tortillas on a baking sheet. Spread vegan cheese or vegan sour cream, tofu, red onion, capers, olives, dill, and tomatoes evenly over both tortillas. Bake at 400°F until the edges of the tortillas turn brown, about 10 to 12 minutes.

Per serving (1/4 of recipe): 317 calories, 15.7 g fat, 2.4 g saturated fat, 42.1% calories from fat, 0 mg cholesterol • 27.3 g protein, 22.3 g carbohydrate, 2.3 g sugar, 3.7 g fiber • 1026 mg sodium, 213 mg calcium, 4.2 mg iron, 5 mg vitamin C, 84 mcg beta-carotene, 0.7 mg vitamin E

HEARTS OF PALM MOQUECA

Horizons, Philadelphia, Pennsylvania

MAKES 6 SERVINGS

1 tablespoon canola oil
1 medium red onion, sliced
2 garlic cloves, crushed
2 14-ounce cans hearts of palm, drained and sliced into rounds
1/2 cup vegetable broth
4 plum tomatoes, chopped
1 14-ounce can coconut milk
1 tablespoon sugar
1/2 teaspoon dry mustard
1/2 teaspoon dried orange zest

1/4 teaspoon ground allspice
1/4 teaspoon ground ginger
1/8 teaspoon salt
1/8 teaspoon black pepper
1/8 teaspoon cayenne pepper
1 green pepper of your choice (green bell, jalapeño, poblano, or habañero depending on desired spiciness)
1/2 cup lightly packed fresh cilantro leaves
6 lime wedges for garnish

Heat oil over medium-high heat in a large skillet or pot. When oil begins to ripple (after about 1 minute), add onion and garlic and stir. Add hearts of palm and sauté the mixture for 2 to 4 minutes. Next, add vegetable broth and bring to a boil. Add tomatoes, coconut milk, sugar, mustard, orange zest, allspice, ginger, salt, black pepper, cayenne, and green pepper. Simmer on medium-low heat until tomatoes have

just started to break down, about 5 to 10 minutes. Remove from heat and stir in cilantro. Squeeze on fresh lime wedges just before eating.

Per serving (1/6 of recipe): 207 calories, 16.7 g fat, 12.5 g saturated fat, 68% calories from fat, 0 mg cholesterol • 3.9 g protein, 15 g carbohydrate, 7.5 g sugar, 3.4 g fiber • 467 mg sodium, 63 mg calcium, 3.4 mg iron, 31.5 mg vitamin C, 216 mcg beta-carotene, 1.1 mg vitamin E

PORTOBELLO MUSHROOM FINGERS WITH CREAMY CORN AND GREEN OLIVE RELISH
Horizons, Philadelphia, Pennsylvania

MAKES 4 TO 6 SERVINGS

PORTOBELLO MUSHROOM FINGERS
3 or 4 large portobello mushroom caps
1/4 cup olive oil
1 teaspoon salt
2 teaspoons black pepper
1 tablespoon balsamic vinegar

CREAMY CORN AND GREEN OLIVE RELISH
1/4 cup green Manzanilla olives (stuffed with pimento or plain)
3/4 cup corn kernels (thawed if using frozen or boiled and cut off the cob if using fresh)
2 tablespoons red onion, chopped
2 tablespoons vegan mayonnaise
1/2 teaspoon Dijon mustard
1 plum tomato, finely chopped

For the mushrooms: Preheat oven to 450°F. Cut mushrooms into 1 1/2-inch strips. In a medium mixing bowl, whisk together oil, salt, black pepper, and balsamic vinegar for marinade. In a mixing bowl, combine the marinade and mushrooms and toss. Lay mushrooms on a baking sheet and roast in preheated oven until the mushrooms have softened and are cooked through, about 7 to 10 minutes.

For the relish: In a food processor, combine olives, corn, and onion and pulse until roughly chopped but not puréed. In a small mixing bowl, toss the corn mixture with mayonnaise, mustard, and tomatoes.

Serve mushroom strips topped with relish.

Per serving (1/4 of recipe): 201 calories, 17.3 g fat, 2.4 g saturated fat, 75.4% calories from fat, 0 mg cholesterol • 3.3 g protein, 11 g carbohydrate, 2.5 g sugar, 2.5 g fiber • 812 mg sodium, 18 mg calcium, 0.9 mg iron, 3.4 mg vitamin C, 101 mcg beta-carotene, 2.8 mg vitamin E

POLENTA CAKES WITH ARUGULA-PARSLEY SALSA
Ottolenghi, London, England

MAKES 6 TO 8 SERVINGS

*D*rawing on an abundance of culinary traditions, with an emphasis on the Mediterranean,
Ottolenghi strives to surprise, creating memorable,
fresh dishes.

ARUGULA-PARSLEY SALSA

1 1/2 cups tightly-packed arugula, plus
  extra leaves for garnish
1/3 cup tightly-packed fresh parsley,
  stems removed
2 tablespoons olive oil
1 garlic clove

1 tablespoon lemon juice
1 tablespoon water, if needed
salt to taste (optional)
freshly ground black pepper to taste
  (optional)

POLENTA CAKES

8 Kalamata olives
2 tablespoons finely chopped chives
1 1/4 cups water
salt, to taste
1/2 cup cornmeal
1 tablespoon vegan margarine

1 tablespoon olive oil
freshly ground black pepper, to taste
2 tablespoons panko or other
  breadcrumbs
vegetable oil for frying

For the salsa: Place arugula, parsley, oil, garlic, and lemon juice
in food processor. Pulse the mixture until it is very roughly
chopped. If it is too thick, add water a little at a time. Adjust
seasonings by adding salt and black pepper, if needed. Pour into
bowl and refrigerate.

For the polenta: Cut olives in half. Press them dry with a paper
towel. Add the dried olives and chives to a food processor, and
pulse the mixture until minced; remove to a medium bowl and
set aside. In a saucepan, bring water to boil with some salt. Add
polenta while stirring constantly with a wooden spoon. Reduce
the heat and keep cooking and stirring for 4 minutes. Take the
polenta off the heat and stir in margarine and olive oil. Adjust
the salt, if necessary, and add lots freshly ground black pepper. The mixture will be very thick. Combine the polenta with
the reserved olives and chives. Place breadcrumbs in a separate
container with sides. While the polenta mixture is still warm,

form walnut-size balls and roll them in the bread crumbs. Chill the polenta cakes in the refrigerator at least 30 to 60 minutes to help them keep their shape while frying.

When ready to serve, heat vegetable oil in a non-stick pan and shallow-fry the polenta cakes until brown, turning them gently so that all sides fry evenly. Drain the cakes on paper towels. Serve the polenta warm or at room temperature on a bed of arugula leaves with the arugula-parsley salsa on the side.

Per serving (1/6 of recipe): 251 calories, 21.7 g fat, 3.1 g saturated fat, 76.1% calories from fat, 0 mg cholesterol • 1.6 g protein, 13.3 g carbohydrate, 0.6 g sugar, 1.1 g fiber • 240 mg sodium, 27 mg calcium, 1.3 mg iron, 6.6 mg vitamin C, 303 mcg beta-carotene, 2.9 mg vitamin E

CASHEW-MUSHROOM PÂTÉ WITH SOURDOUGH TOAST POINTS

Lovin' Spoonfuls, Tucson, Arizona

MAKES 8 SERVINGS

*A*fter a day in the Arizona desert, cool down at Lovin' Spoonfuls. You'll find delicious, healthful dining in a welcoming atmosphere and a wide variety of tasty, beautifully-presented dishes.

1 1/2 tablespoons non-hydrogenated vegan margarine
4 cups mushrooms, sliced
1/4 cup onion, coarsely chopped
1 garlic clove, minced
1 teaspoon curry powder
1/4 teaspoon salt
1/8 teaspoon ground cumin

1/2 cup roasted cashews
2 teaspoons chunky peanut butter
2 teaspoons cooking sherry
2 tablespoons fresh parsley, chopped, for garnish
3 roasted red pepper strips, for garnish
1 sourdough baguette

Heat margarine in a large skillet over medium heat. Add mushrooms, onion, garlic, curry powder, salt, and cumin. Sauté until mushrooms are tender and most of the liquid has evaporated, about 10 to 12 minutes. Transfer vegetables to a food processor and add cashews and peanut butter. Purée mixture until it is relatively smooth. Transfer to a bowl and chill for at least two hours.

Make toast points by diagonally slicing baguette and toasting until light brown. Scoop pâté into the center of a plate or bowl, sprinkle with parsley and decorate with red pepper strips. Surround pâté with toast points and serve.

Per serving (1/8 of recipe): 203 calories, 7.6 g fat, 1.5 g saturated fat, 32.1% calories from fat. 0 mg cholesterol • 7.2 g protein, 27.8 g carbohydrate, 4.1 g sugar, 2.1 g fiber • 395 mg sodium, 29 mg calcium, 2.6 mg iron, 4.4 mg vitamin C, 77 mcg beta-carotene, 0.4 mg vitamin E

Soups

CURRY CARROT SOUP

Lovin' Spoonfuls, Tucson, Arizona

MAKES 4 SERVINGS

1 tablespoon olive oil
1 1/2 tablespoons minced ginger
1 medium onion, chopped
5 cups vegetable broth
6 carrots, sliced
3/4 cup coconut milk *Lite*

2 teaspoons curry powder
2 teaspoons fresh basil, chopped
1 teaspoon fresh cilantro, chopped
2 garlic cloves, minced
1/4 cup fresh parsley, chopped, for
garnish

Combine olive oil, ginger, onion, broth, carrots, coconut milk, curry powder, basil, cilantro, and garlic in a medium stockpot. Bring to a boil, reduce heat, and simmer on medium-low heat until carrots are tender, about 15 to 20 minutes. Let mixture cool, then place in a blender and process until smooth, in two batches, if necessary. Serve garnished with parsley.

Per serving (1/4 of recipe): 179 calories, 12.7 g fat, 8.4 g saturated fat, 60.1% calories from fat, 0 mg cholesterol • 2.1 g protein, 17.3 g carbohydrate, 9.6 g sugar, 3.8 g fiber • 1233 mg sodium, 53 mg calcium, 1.3 mg iron, 10.8 mg vitamin C, 7516 mcg beta-carotene, 1.7 mg vitamin E

Early Girl Tomato Soup
La Toque, Napa, California

MAKES 6 SERVINGS

*L*a Toque, in the gorgeous Napa Valley, serves seasonal dishes that harmonize with the wines of the region on its elegant outdoor patio.

3 pounds Early Girl tomatoes or other ripe tomatoes
1 cup extra-virgin olive oil, divided
1/2 large yellow onion, peeled and finely chopped

2 garlic cloves, chopped
salt, to taste
freshly ground white pepper, to taste

Bring a pot of water to a boil. Prepare a separate medium bowl of ice water and set aside.

Remove cores from tomatoes. Using a paring knife, cut a small X on the non-core end of each tomato. Place tomatoes in boiling water just long enough to loosen the skins, about 30 to 45

seconds, then remove immediately with a slotted spoon or strainer and place in prepared bowl of ice water to cool. Remove tomatoes from ice water and peel (the skins will slip off easily). Discard the skins, squeeze out seeds and juice, and strain tomatoes, reserving all juice and tomato pulp. Set pulp and juice aside.

Heat 1/2 cup oil in a non-reactive thick bottomed pan over medium heat. Add onion and cook until tender (do not brown). Add tomato pulp and juice and garlic. Season with salt and white pepper. Bring to a boil, then lower heat to a gentle simmer. Cook, partially covered, for about 1 hour, stirring frequently. Be careful not to scorch the bottom of the pan. Remove mixture to a blender and purée with remaining 1/2 cup oil. Strain to remove any seeds. Taste soup and add salt and black pepper, if needed. If soup is too thick, add a splash of water.

Chill soup before serving.

Per serving (1/6 of recipe): 354 calories, 36.2 g fat, 5 g saturated fat, 90.4% calories from fat, 0 mg cholesterol • 1.8 g protein, 8 g carbohydrate, 4.5 g sugar, 1.3 g fiber • 166 mg sodium, 23 mg calcium, 1.4 mg iron, 37.6 mg vitamin C, 472 mcg beta-carotene, 6 mg vitamin E

PARADAJZ ČORBA
Taphana Restaurant, Ulcinj, Montenegro

MAKES 3 SERVINGS

*P*erched above the Mediterranean near the Montenegro-Albania border, Taphana serves delicious traditional cuisine as the sea breezes carry ancient history into its modern interior.

4 fresh tomatoes, chopped
1 cup vegetable broth
1 cup cooked brown rice
1/2 zucchini, finely chopped

1 tablespoon fresh cilantro, finely chopped
1/2 teaspoon green chili, finely chopped
juice of 1/4 lemon

Combine all ingredients in a pot. Bring to a boil, then stir and simmer for about 10 minutes. Serve hot.

Per serving (1/3 of recipe): 108 calories, 0.8 g fat, 0.1 g saturated fat, 6% calories from fat,0 mg cholesterol • 3.3 g protein, 23.2 g carbohydrate, 5.4 g sugar, 3.6 g fiber • 334 mg sodium, 29 mg calcium, 1.4 mg iron, 37.1 mg vitamin C, 718 mcg beta-carotene, 0.8 mg vitamin E

GALANGAL COCONUT SOUP

Pun Pun, Mae Taeng, Thailand

MAKES 4 SERVINGS

*N*estled inside the Suan Dok temple's courtyard, the Pun Pun Organic Restaurant serves delicious vegetarian Thai food using fruits and vegetables grown by local organic farmers.

4 cups vegetable broth
2 cups coconut milk
16 ounces firm tofu, cut into 1/2-inch
  cubes
12 shiitake mushrooms
12 canned straw mushrooms
12 oyster mushrooms
1/2 cup chopped coconut shoots or
  carrot (1/4-inch cubes)
1/2 cup chopped chayote squash or
  pumpkin (1/4-inch cubes)

4 kaffir lime leaves, very thinly sliced
4 teaspoons lemongrass, very
  thinly sliced
8 teaspoons fresh galangal or
  ginger, very thinly sliced
1 to 4 teaspoons chili paste
1/4 cup reduced-sodium soy sauce
1/4 cup lemon or lime juice
1/2 cup fresh cilantro, chopped, for
  garnish

Combine broth and coconut milk in a large pot over medium heat. Bring to a boil, then add tofu, mushrooms, coconut shoots or carrot, chayote squash or pumpkin, kaffir lime leaves, lemongrass, and galangal or ginger. Return to a boil and cook until mushrooms are tender, about 3 minutes. Add chili paste and keep soup at a boil until all vegetables are cooked. Remove soup from heat and add soy sauce and lemon or lime juice. Garnish with cilantro.

Per serving (1/4 of recipe): 398 calories, 29.1 g fat, 22.1 g saturated fat, 61.1% calories from fat, 0 mg cholesterol • 15.5 g protein, 27.3 g carbohydrate, 10.2 g sugar, 5.5 g fiber • 1609 mg sodium, 253 mg calcium, 4.4 mg iron, 8.3 mg vitamin C, 338 mcg beta-carotene, 0.3 mg vitamin E

CHILLED CANARY MELON AND GREEN ZEBRA TOMATO SOUP WITH TOFU CARDAMOM CREAM
Millennium Restaurant, San Francisco, California

MAKES 6 SERVINGS

San Francisco's legendary restaurant delivers an elegant dining experience and an extraordinary menu. Every dish is a delight—without a speck of animal ingredients.

TOFU CARDAMOM CREAM
1/2 12.3-ounce package soft silken tofu
1 teaspoon white miso
1/2 teaspoon ground cardamom
1/4 teaspoon salt
1/4 cup water

CANARY MELON AND GREEN ZEBRA TOMATO SOUP
4 cups Canary melon flesh (can substitute orange melon flesh)
1 cup Green Zebra tomatoes (can substitute gold or red tomatoes), seeded, chopped
1 tablespoon fresh ginger, minced
2 cups water
juice of 1 lime
1 teaspoon raw sugar or agave nectar
1/4 teaspoon cayenne pepper
salt, to taste
2 tablespoons small spearmint or peppermint leaves, for garnish

For the cream: Place tofu, miso, cardamom, salt, and water in a blender and blend until smooth.

For the soup: Place melon, tomatoes, ginger, water, lime juice, sugar or agave nectar, cayenne, and salt in a blender and process until smooth. Adjust salt to taste. Refrigerate until well chilled.

Top each serving with Tofu Cardamom Cream. Scatter mint leaves over the top.

Per serving (1/6 of recipe): 68 calories, 1.2 g fat, 0.2 g saturated fat, 15.1% calories from fat, 0 mg cholesterol • 3.4 g protein, 12.3 g carbohydrate, 10.4 g sugar, 1.6 g fiber • 316 mg sodium, 31 mg calcium, 0.9 mg iron, 44.6 mg vitamin C, 2327 mcg beta-carotene, 0.4 mg vitamin E

Leek and Basmati Rice Soup

Greens Restaurant, San Francisco, California

MAKES 8 SERVINGS

*L*ocated in a converted warehouse at San Francisco's historic Fort Mason, Greens has an airy, art-filled dining room and floor to ceiling windows that offer sweeping views of the Marina, the Golden Gate Bridge, and the Marin headlands.

LEEK STOCK

1 yellow onion, sliced
10 garlic cloves, unpeeled, crushed with the side of a knife blade
1 teaspoon salt
3 green leek tops, coarsely chopped and washed
2 medium carrots, cut into large pieces
1 celery rib, cut into large pieces

1 large potato, sliced
1 bay leaf
2 fresh sage leaves
5 fresh parsley sprigs
5 fresh thyme sprigs
2 fresh marjoram or oregano sprigs
8 cups cold water

SOUP

2 tablespoons light olive oil
4 or 5 large leeks, white parts only, cut in half lengthwise, thinly sliced, and washed (about 9 cups)
salt
white pepper
6 garlic cloves, finely chopped
1/2 cup dry white wine
1 medium carrot, chopped (about 3/4 cup)
2 celery ribs, chopped (about 3/4 cup)

1/4 cup dry basmati rice
fresh herb sachet (1 bay leaf, 4 thyme sprigs, 5 parsley sprigs, 1 sage leaf, and 2 marjoram sprigs tied in a cheesecloth or bundled and tied together)
1 recipe (about 7 cups) Leek Stock, divided
1 tablespoon fresh parsley, chopped
1 tablespoon fresh chives, chopped
1 tablespoon fresh marjoram, chopped

For the stock: Heat onion and garlic in a soup pot or stockpot with salt and 1/4 inch water. Cover pot and steam for 15 minutes over medium heat. Add the rest of the ingredients and bring stock to a boil, then turn down the heat and simmer, uncovered, for 40 to 45 minutes. Pour through a strainer and discard the vegetables. Set aside.

For the soup: Heat oil in a soup pot over medium heat. Add leeks, 1 tablespoon salt, and a few pinches white pepper. Stir leeks, coating them with oil, then cover pot, reduce heat to low and cook for about 10 minutes, until leeks are wilted.

Add garlic and sauté for another minute or two, then add wine and cook for another minute or two, until wine evaporates. Add carrot, celery, rice, 1/2 teaspoon salt, herb sachet, and 4 cups Leek Stock. Bring soup to a boil, then reduce the heat, cover, and simmer for 15 minutes. Add remaining 3 cups Leek Stock and season soup to taste with salt and white pepper. Remove herb sachet and add parsley, chives, and marjoram just before serving.

Per serving (1/8 of recipe): 98 calories, 3.6 g fat, 0.5 g saturated fat, 32.3% calories from fat, 0 mg cholesterol • 1.2 g protein, 13.8 g carbohydrate, 4 g sugar, 1.2 g fiber • 1452 mg sodium, 39 mg calcium, 1.1 mg iron, 4.9 mg vitamin C, 885 mcg beta-carotene, 0.9 mg vitamin E

CARROT GINGER SOUP
Sublime, Fort Lauderdale, Florida

MAKES 6 SERVINGS

The inspiration of Nanci Alexander, Sublime is a world-class experience in every way, from its gorgeous interior, with waterfalls and original Peter Max paintings, to its unequaled award-winning cuisine. Everything from tempting appetizers to phenomenal desserts is prepared with no animal ingredients, so every bite is a treat for the palate, the waistline, and our animal friends.

1/4 cup canola oil
5 cups carrots, sliced
1 cup shallots, sliced
1 tablespoon fenugreek seeds
1 tablespoon fennel seeds
3 cups vegetable broth

3 cups coconut milk
3 tablespoons ginger, minced
kosher salt, to taste
ground black pepper, to taste
chives, finely sliced, for garnish

Sauté carrots and shallots in oil in a large stockpot until tender, about 5 to 10 minutes. Add fenugreek and fennel seeds to toast. Cover carrots with broth and simmer until very soft and dark orange. Remove from heat and add coconut milk. Add ginger. Purée the mixture in a blender until smooth and creamy. Season with salt and black pepper. Garnish with chives when serving.

Per serving (1/6 of recipe): 368 calories, 33.3 g fat, 21.8 g saturated fat, 76.9% calories from fat, 0 mg cholesterol • 3.7 g protein, 19.3 g carbohydrate, 11.1 g sugar, 5.5 g fiber • 689 mg sodium, 68 mg calcium, 2.2 mg iron, 14.1 mg vitamin C, 8083 mcg beta-carotene, 2.7 mg vitamin E

BUTTERNUT SQUASH AND KIDNEY BEAN POTAGE

Seed Café, Venice, California

MAKES 4 SERVINGS

$\mathcal{S}$eed Café specializes in organic macrobiotic dishes that are healthy, delicious, and eye-catching. Don't be surprised if you run into a movie star or two.

2 tablespoons olive oil
1 yellow onion, finely chopped
1 butternut squash
2 carrots, finely chopped
2 cups water
1/4 teaspoon sea salt

1/4 teaspoon curry powder
1 tablespoon white miso
1/2 cup unsweetened rice milk
1 15-ounce can red kidney beans, undrained

Peel squash with a vegetable peeler, slice in half, and remove seeds. Coarsely chop squash and set aside. Warm oil in a medium saucepan. Add onion and lightly sauté for a few minutes. Add squash, carrots, and water, and simmer for a few minutes. Add salt and curry powder. Bring to a boil, reduce heat, and simmer for 20 minutes. Transfer the mixture to a blender. Add miso and rice milk and purée until creamy. Transfer the purée to a large bowl or pot. Heat undrained beans in a small pot or saucepan, then drain and gently stir into soup. Serve.

Per serving (1/4 of recipe): 288 calories, 7.9 g fat, 1.1 g saturated fat, 24.2% calories from fat, 0 mg cholesterol • 9.7 g protein, 49.8 g carbohydrate, 13.4 g sugar, 9.6 g fiber • 516 mg sodium, 173 mg calcium, 3.5 mg iron, 41.6 mg vitamin C, 13,700 mcg beta-carotene, 4.6 mg vitamin E

MASOOR DAL SOUP

Rajput Indian Cuisine, Norfolk, Virginia

MAKES 3 TO 4 SERVINGS

$\mathcal{A}$ny restaurant would be proud to feature carefully pre-pared, authentic Indian cuisine. But Paul Chhabra's creativity has carried him several steps further. Modifying traditional recipes to omit animal products and oils and incorporate novel ingredients, he has sparked a whole new way of thinking about Indian food.

1 cup dry masoor dal (red lentils)
3 cups water, plus more if needed
1 teaspoon cumin seeds
1 teaspoon grated fresh ginger, soaked in water
5 curry leaves (can substitute 2 bay leaves or double amount of cumin seeds)

1/4 teaspoon turmeric
1/4 teaspoon asafetida (optional)
1/4 teaspoon salt (or to taste) *Table tast*
1 tablespoon lemon juice
2 tablespoons fresh cilantro, chopped

Add masoor dal and 3 cups water to a pot. Bring to a boil, then simmer until soft, about 15 minutes. Set aside.

Heat a medium non-stick pan and add cumin seeds. Toast on medium heat for about 1 minute, being careful not to burn them. Add drained ginger and curry leaves and cook the mixture for 2 minutes. Add turmeric and asafetida, if using. Stir and immediately add cooked dal (lentils). Add water if necessary to moisten lentils. If you prefer a thinner consistency, add up to 1/2 cup water.

Simmer soup for about 10 minutes and add salt to taste. Just before serving, add lemon juice and garnish with cilantro.

Per serving (1/3 of recipe): 209 calories, 0.9 g fat, 0.1 g saturated fat, 3.4% calories from fat, 0 mg cholesterol • 16.1 g protein, 36.4 g carbohydrate, 0.8 g sugar, 10.5 g fiber • 203 mg sodium, 41 mg calcium, 6.4 mg iron, 4.2 mg vitamin C, 40 mcg beta-carotene, 0.2 mg vitamin E

SOPA DE VERDURAS
La More, Cancún, Mexico

MAKES 5 SERVINGS

*T*he Yucatan peninsula is home to the Maya civilization, where traditional health-ful cuisine was based mainly on corn, beans, squash, and other plant foods. Just as the dazzling Maya pyramids near Cancún have been all but buried over time, Maya foods have been crowded out by the offerings of steak houses and sports bars. And yet, smack in the middle of Cancún's tour-ist zone, La More pays homage to simple healthful traditions.

1 tablespoon olive oil
1/4 cup garlic, minced
1 cup onion, chopped
1 1/2 teaspoons salt
1 1/2 teaspoons black pepper
1 1/2 teaspoons cayenne pepper
1 cup blended fresh tomatoes
1 cup fresh or frozen corn kernels
1 cup carrots, chopped

1 potato, peeled and chopped
1 cup pumpkin, peeled and chopped
1 cup chayote or butternut squash, peeled and chopped
3 cups water
2 cups chard leaf strips (stems removed)
1 cup Brussels sprouts, chopped
5 tablespoons fresh cilantro, chopped

Place oil into a large pot over medium heat. Add garlic and onion and cook and stir until they begin to brown. Add salt, black pepper, and cayenne and cook for one minute. Add tomatoes, corn, carrots, potato, pumpkin, and squash. Once vegetables start to become tender, add water, chard, and Brussels sprouts. Simmer until chard and Brussels sprouts are tender, about 5 minutes, adding more water if needed. Add cilantro immediately before serving.

Per serving (1/5 of recipe): 155 calories, 3.5 g fat, 0.5 g saturated fat, 19.9% calories from fat, 0 mg cholesterol • 4.9 g protein, 29.9 g carbohydrate, 7.7 g sugar, 6.2 g fiber • 772 mg sodium, 67 mg calcium, 2.2 mg iron, 32.7 mg vitamin C, 3342 mcg beta-carotene, 2.4 mg vitamin E

VEGETABLE SOUP ALLA NILDE

Da Antonio, Brunate, Italy

MAKES 6 SERVINGS

*T*o get there, you'll need to find your way to Italy's Lake Como, and then ride the funicular up the mountainside. But you'll be glad you did. Have a cool drink on the terrace under the trees. A homemade Italian meal awaits you.

2 tablespoons olive oil
1/2 medium onion, finely chopped
1/4 cup leek, finely chopped
1 garlic clove
2 tablespoons dry white wine
8 cups water
salt, to taste
1/4 cup fresh basil, roughly chopped
1 tablespoon fresh sage, chopped
1 tablespoon fresh rosemary, chopped
1 1/2 cups potatoes, chopped
3/4 cup carrots, chopped

3/4 cup celery, chopped
3/4 cup fresh or frozen green peas
1/2 cup canned borlotti beans or
    black beans, drained
1/2 cup canned garbanzo beans.
    drained
1/3 cup canned cannellini beans,
    drained
1/4 cup dry lentils
pinch sugar
freshly ground black pepper, to taste

In a small frying pan, heat olive oil. Add onion, leek, and whole garlic clove and sauté. When onion becomes golden, add white wine and then remove from heat and set aside.

Place water in a separate large pot with salt, basil, sage, and rosemary. Remove garlic clove from sautéed onion mixture and add to pot. Bring water to a boil. Add cooked onion and leek, potatoes, carrots, celery, peas, beans, and lentils. Cook until potatoes and carrots are tender, about 15 minutes. Add sugar.

Serve soup in a bowl with freshly ground black pepper.

Per serving (1/6 of recipe): 185 calories, 5.2 g fat, 0.7 g saturated fat, 24.9% calories from fat, 0 mg cholesterol • 7.4 g protein, 27.2 g carbohydrate, 3.1 g sugar, 6.8 g fiber • 256 mg sodium, 67 mg calcium, 3 mg iron, 10 mg vitamin C, 1412 mcg beta-carotene, 1.2 mg vitamin E

Salads

ROMAINE HEARTS WITH AVOCADO, JÍCAMA, AND ORANGE

Greens Restaurant, San Francisco, California

MAKES 4 SERVINGS

CITRUS-CUMIN VINAIGRETTE

3 tablespoons light olive oil	1/8 teaspoon cumin seeds, toasted
2 tablespoons fresh orange juice	and ground
1 tablespoon champagne vinegar	1/2 teaspoon minced orange zest
1/4 teaspoon salt	

SALAD

2 heads romaine lettuce (8 to 10 cups hearts)	1 teaspoon champagne vinegar
1 large navel orange	1/2 teaspoon salt
1/2 medium jícama, about 1/4 pound	1/2 teaspoon cayenne pepper
3 tablespoons fresh orange juice	1 avocado
	freshly ground black pepper, to taste

For the vinaigrette: Combine oil, orange juice, vinegar, salt, and cumin seeds in a blender. Blend, then whisk in the zest. Set aside.

For the salad: Trim the base of the romaine, discarding tough outer leaves and saving light green inner leaves or hearts. Cut the larger leaves in half down the length of the rib; cut into quarters if long and keep the smaller leaves whole. Wash lettuce and dry it in a spinner, then wrap in a damp towel and refrigerate.

Using a sharp knife, remove peel and white pith from orange, slicing a piece off the top and bottom, then working down the sides. Slice orange in half through the stem end and remove seeds or pith in the center. Slice across the orange, making 1/4-inch half-moons. Set aside.

Peel jícama and slice it into thin matchsticks, about 2 inches long. Combine orange juice, vinegar, salt, and cayenne in a plastic container with a lid. Add the jícama and marinate for 10 to 15 minutes. Drain and set aside.

Just before serving, cut avocado in half, peel it, and thinly slice it on a slight diagonal.

Place lettuce, orange slices, drained jícama, and prepared vinaigrette in a large bowl and toss until the leaves are coated. Add avocado and toss again, taking care not to break avocado slices. Sprinkle the salad with freshly ground black pepper and serve.

Per serving (1/4 of recipe): 221 calories, 15.8 g fat, 2.2 g saturated fat, 62% calories from fat, 0 mg cholesterol • 2.9 g protein, 20 g carbohydrate, 6 g sugar, 9.5 g fiber • 235 mg sodium, 67 mg calcium, 1.9 mg iron, 70.7 mg vitamin C, 3356 mcg beta-carotene, 3.2 mg vitamin E

SPRING GREENS SALAD WITH BLOOD ORANGE VINAIGRETTE

VegiTerranean, Akron, Ohio

MAKES 6 SERVINGS

*O*wned by Chrissie Hynde of The Pretenders, VegiTerranean is a rock star in the restaurant world.

1/4 cup blood orange juice
1/4 cup canola oil
2 tablespoons agave nectar
1 1/2 tablespoons white balsamic
   vinegar

1 1/2 tablespoons finely chopped
   shallots
1 teaspoon salt
2 teaspoons black pepper
6 cups spring greens

Whisk juice, oil, vinegar, agave nectar, shallots, salt, and black pepper together in a small bowl. Toss with greens and serve.

Per serving (1/6 of recipe): 122 calories, 9.3 g fat, 0.7 g saturated fat, 67% calories from fat, 0 mg cholesterol • 1.1 g protein, 9.7 g carbohydrate, 5.9 g sugar, 1.3 g fiber • 414 mg sodium, 47 mg calcium, 1.2 mg iron, 14.3 mg vitamin C, 1880 mcg beta-carotene, 2 mg vitamin E

CAESAR SALAD
Lovin' Spoonfuls, Tucson, Arizona

MAKES 6 SERVINGS

1/2 cup olive oil
1/2 cup vegan mayonnaise
1/4 cup pine nuts
2 garlic cloves
2 tablespoons nutritional yeast
2 tablespoons Dijon mustard
1 tablespoon lemon juice
1/2 tablespoon vegan Worcestershire
  sauce

1/2 tablespoon onion powder
1 teaspoon garlic salt
1/4 teaspoon kelp powder
8 cups romaine lettuce hearts,
  chopped
1 cup vegan parmesan cheese
  (optional)

Combine oil, vegan mayonnaise, pine nuts, garlic, nutritional yeast, mustard, lemon juice, vegan Worcestershire sauce, onion powder, garlic salt, and kelp powder in a blender and process until smooth. Toss with lettuce and sprinkle with vegan parmesan, if using.

Per serving (1/6 of recipe): 278 calories, 26.8 g fat, 3.7 g saturated fat, 84.7% calories from fat, 0 mg cholesterol • 4.2 g protein, 7.5 g carbohydrate, 2.6 g sugar, 2.8 g fiber • 464 mg sodium, 37 mg calcium, 1.4 mg iron, 16.9 mg vitamin C, 2211 mcg beta-carotene, 4.5 mg vitamin E

TOMATO CARPACCIO
Sublime, Fort Lauderdale, Florida

MAKES 4 SERVINGS

2 large heirloom tomatoes (about 2
  pounds), sliced paper-thin
3 tablespoons extra-virgin olive oil
1 teaspoon cracked black pepper

1/2 cup capers
2 cups baby greens or microgreens
1 cup basil leaves

On four chilled plates, arrange sliced tomatoes in concentric circles until the plates are covered. Drizzle with oil and season with black pepper. Scatter capers and greens around the tomatoes. Top with basil leaves and serve.

Per serving (1/4 of recipe): 138 calories, 10.8 g fat, 1.5 g saturated fat, 69% calories from fat, 0 mg cholesterol • 2.9 g protein, 10.3 g carbohydrate, 6.1 g sugar, 3.8 g fiber • 529 mg sodium, 54 mg calcium, 1.6 mg iron, 32.5 mg vitamin C, 1964 mcg beta-carotene, 3 mg vitamin E

SUPER MIX
SALAD

Pun Pun, Mae Taeng, Thailand

MAKES 6 SERVINGS

SALAD

4 cups baby spinach
2 cups mixed salad greens
1 cup purple cabbage, shredded
1 cup carrot, shredded
1/2 cup raw beet, shredded
1/2 cup jícama, shredded
1 apple, thinly sliced
1 cup fresh pineapple, chopped

1 cup strawberries, sliced
1/2 cup grapes, sliced
1/2 cup canned kidney beans, drained
1/4 cup pumpkin seeds, roasted
1 tablespoon white sesame seeds
1 tablespoon black sesame seeds
1 teaspoon black pepper

DRESSING

3 garlic cloves
water
2 tablespoons sugar
1 1/2 teaspoons mustard powder
3/4 cup baby carrots. chopped

1 1/2 teaspoons olive oil
1 tablespoon sesame oil
3 1/2 tablespoons apple cider vinegar
3 tablespoons soy sauce
2 1/2 tablespoons lemon or lime juice

For the salad: Pile spinach and greens on a large platter. Top with cabbage, carrot, beet, and jícama. Arrange apple, pine-apple, strawberries, grapes, and beans on top of salad and around the platter. Sprinkle with seeds and black pepper. Set aside.

For the dressing: Blend garlic in blender with 1 tablespoon water. Add sugar and enough additional water to cover ingredients and blend until smooth. Then add mustard powder and carrots. Blend until smooth. Pour into bowl and add oils, vinegar, soy sauce, and lemon or lime juice. Stir and add more water if dressing consistency is too thick.

Serve salad with dressing on the side.

Per serving (1/6 of recipe): 228 calories, 10 g fat, 1.6 g saturated fat, 37.4% calories from fat, 0 mg cholesterol • 7.9 g protein, 30.8 g carbohydrate, 17.1 g sugar, 6.5 g fiber • 601 mg sodium, 79 mg calcium, 3.7 mg iron, 54.7 mg vitamin C, 4719 mcg beta-carotene, 1.8 mg vitamin E

CRANBERRY-SAGE ARUGULA SALAD
WITH ROASTED FRUIT

Candle 79, New York, New York

MAKES 6 SERVINGS

*N*ew York's vegetarian, organic, and delicious Candle 79 has been the dining destination for a devoted clientele, including health-conscious families, romantic couples, and celebrities.

DRESSING

1/2 cup grapeseed oil, divided
2 shallots, finely chopped
1/2 cup fresh cranberries
3 sprigs fresh sage

1 teaspoon sea salt
1/4 teaspoon black pepper
pinch of ground cinnamon

SALAD

2 beets, scrubbed
2 pears
2 tablespoons extra-virgin olive oil
1 cup pecans

1 fennel bulb
6 fresh figs, halved
1 pound baby arugula

For the dressing: Heat 2 tablespoons grapeseed oil in a small saucepan. Add shallots and fresh cranberries and sauté until soft. Allow to cool. Combine shallots, cranberries, sage, remaining 6 tablespoons grapeseed oil, salt, black pepper, and cinnamon in a blender and process until smooth. Set aside.

For the salad: Preheat oven to 350°F.

Wrap beets in foil and roast until tender, about 45 to 60 minutes. Allow to cool, then peel, slice, and set aside.

Cut pears into halves. Place halves on a roasting pan, drizzle with olive oil, and roast in the oven until tender, about 10 to 15 minutes. Remove from oven, cool, and slice. Set aside.

Arrange pecans on a sheet pan in a single layer and roast for 6 minutes. Remove from oven and set aside.

Cut off base of fennel bulb and quarter. Remove core from each quarter and run a vegetable peeler lengthwise down the cut side of each quarter to produce shavings.

Place prepared beets, pears, pecans, and fennel in a large mixing bowl. Add arugula and toss. Drizzle with dressing and serve.

Per serving (1/6 of recipe): 411 calories, 35.4 g fat, 3.5 g saturated fat, 74.6% calories from fat, 0 mg cholesterol • 4.9 g protein, 24.7 g carbohydrate, 11.2 g sugar, 7.3 g fiber • 445 mg sodium, 184 mg calcium, 2.4 mg iron, 21.9 mg vitamin C, 1207 mcg beta-carotene, 6.7 mg vitamin E

PORCINI MUSHROOM SALAD WITH HAZELNUTS AND WHITE CELERY

Navedano, Como, Italy

MAKES 3 SERVINGS

*I*n Lake Como, near Milan, Navedano serves up carefully prepared dishes using the freshest local ingredients.

1/2 cup fresh porcini or oyster mushrooms (can substitute reconstituted dried porcini)
1/4 teaspoon salt
1/2 teaspoon black pepper

2 tablespoons extra-virgin olive oil
1/4 cup julienned white or green celery
1/4 cup raw hazelnuts, crushed

Clean and chop mushrooms. Toss mushrooms with salt, black pepper, and oil. Place mushrooms in the center of a dish and top with celery and hazelnuts.

Per serving (1/3 of recipe): 148 calories, 14.9 g fat, 1.7 g saturated fat, 87.1% calories from fat, 0 mg cholesterol • 2 g protein, 3 g carbohydrate, 0.8 g sugar, 1.5 g fiber • 206 mg sodium, 16 mg calcium, 0.8 mg iron, 0.9 mg vitamin C, 28 mcg beta-carotene, 2.8 mg vitamin E

Main Dishes

PARSNIP DUMPLINGS IN BROTH

Ottolenghi, London, England

MAKES 4 SERVINGS

BROTH

2 tablespoons olive oil
2 carrots, peeled and cut into sticks
4 celery stalks, cut into chunks
5 garlic cloves, peeled
1 onion, quartered
1/2 celeriac, peeled and cut roughly

3 fresh thyme sprigs
2 small bunches fresh parsley
10 peppercorns
2 bay leaves
3 tablespoons frozen green peas
6 to 8 cups cold water

DUMPLINGS

2 2/3 cups peeled and chopped
    potatoes
1 1/2 cups peeled and chopped
    parsnips
1 garlic clove, peeled
2 tablespoons vegan margarine
pinch white pepper

1/2 cup self-rising flour
1/3 cup semolina
vegan egg replacer, such as Ener-G
    Egg Replacer, equivalent to 1 egg
pinch salt
2 tablespoons fresh parsley,
    chopped, for garnish

For the broth: In a large stock pot, heat oil over medium heat. Add carrots, celery, garlic, onion, and celeriac and sauté until they color lightly. Add thyme, parsley, peppercorns, and bay leaves and cover with water. Simmer for up to 2 hours, skimming the surface as needed. Make sure you have at least 3 cups of broth remaining. Strain broth through a fine sieve and set aside. Save about half the carrots that have been strained out of the broth; discard remaining vegetables.

For the dumplings: Bring a large pot of water to a boil. Add potatoes, parsnips, and garlic, return to a boil, and cook until soft, about 20 minutes. Drain well. In a separate large pan, heat the margarine over medium heat. Add cooked potato mixture and sauté to remove all moisture, about 5 minutes. While the mixture is hot, mash by hand. Transfer to a large bowl and stir in flour, semolina, egg replacer, salt, and white pepper. Cover with plastic wrap and chill in the refrigerator for 30 to 60 minutes.

Return prepared broth to the stove and add the reserved cooked carrots. Reheat on medium heat until broth is warm, about 5 minutes. Add peas 2 minutes before serving.

To form the dumplings, bring another pot of water to a light simmer, dip a teaspoon in heated water and then use it to spoon out dumpling mix into the water. Allow dumplings to come up to the surface, cook 30 seconds, and then remove from water. Place cooked dumplings in hot broth, garnish with chopped parsley, and serve immediately.

Per serving (1/4 of recipe): 294 calories, 6.5 g fat, 1.3 g saturated fat, 19.4% calories from fat, 0 mg cholesterol • 6.7 g protein, 54.3 g carbohydrate, 6 g sugar, 6.4 g fiber • 373 mg sodium, 115 mg calcium, 2.4 mg iron, 17.8 mg vitamin C, 1372 mcg beta-carotene, 1.1 mg vitamin E

FAJAS DE NOPALES
La More, Cancún, Mexico

MAKES 4 SERVINGS

*N*opales—the leaves of the prickly pear cactus—can be found fresh or canned in many Latin American grocery stores or in the international aisle of your local supermarket.

1 tablespoon olive oil
3 garlic cloves, minced
1/2 onion, chopped
1 cup nopales (drained if canned), peeled, de-thorned, and chopped
1 tomato, chopped
1 red bell pepper, chopped
1/2 cup fresh cilantro, chopped
1 tablespoon soy sauce
2 teaspoons black pepper, or to taste
8 corn tortillas
1 avocado, sliced
1/4 cup vegan sour cream (optional)

Heat oil in a medium skillet over medium heat. Add garlic and onion and sauté until tender, about 5 minutes. Add nopales and cook until tender, about 5 minutes. Add tomato and red pepper. Once red pepper is cooked al dente, about 5 minutes, remove from heat and add cilantro, soy sauce, and black pepper. Serve the fajas on warm corn tortillas with a garnish of avocado and vegan sour cream, if using.

Per serving (1/4 of recipe): 221 calories, 10.2 g fat, 1.4 g saturated fat, 39.2% calories from fat, 0 mg cholesterol • 4.9 g protein, 31.1 g carbohydrate, 4 g sugar, 6.5 g fiber • 259 mg sodium, 98 mg calcium, 1.8 mg iron, 62.1 mg vitamin C, 672 mcg beta-carotene, 2 mg vitamin E

STEAMED CORN AND ARAME CAKES
WITH GINGER-PEACH SALSA

Millennium, San Francisco, California

MAKES 6 SERVINGS

GINGER-PEACH SALSA

1 garlic clove, minced
2 teaspoons fresh ginger, minced
1 teaspoon fermented black beans,
 minced
1/8 teaspoon red pepper, crushed

2 tomatoes, seeded and chopped
2 peaches, peeled and chopped
juice of 1 lime
1/4 cup fresh cilantro, finely chopped

CORN CAKES

1/2 yellow onion, finely chopped
water, as needed
1/4 cup soaked arame seaweed
2 kaffir lime leaves, thinly sliced
1 teaspoon tamari

2 cups fresh corn kernels
1/2 cup cornmeal, plus more as
 needed
1/2 cup fresh parsley leaves
salt, to taste

For the ginger-peach salsa: Heat a non-stick skillet over high heat. Add garlic and stir until it starts to brown. Add ginger, black beans, pepper flakes, and tomatoes. Stir and sauté until tomatoes start to get soft and fall apart. Remove from heat and add peaches, lime juice, and cilantro.

For the corn cakes: In a non-stick skillet over medium heat, soften onion with just enough water to barely cover until water evaporates. Add arame, lime leaves, and tamari. Stir and heat through, then place in a mixing bowl and set aside

Place corn in a food processor. Process until corn is minced. Add

flour and continue to process until mixture forms a soft dough. Fold into onion mixture. Fold in parsley and add salt to taste.

Set up a steamer. Using about 1/4 cup batter per cake, place some batter in the steamer tray and press to form 1/2- to 2/3-inch thick cakes (if the steamer has large perforations, line it with lettuce, cabbage leaves, or banana leaf). Cover and steam for 15 minutes. The cakes will still be a little soft. Turn off heat and let cakes rest another 10 minutes before serving.

Serve each cake with a generous spoonful of the ginger-peach salsa.

Per serving (1/6 of recipe): 121 calories, 0.8 g fat, 0.1 g saturated fat, 5.2% calories from fat, 0 mg cholesterol • 3.3 g protein, 27.7 g carbohydrate, 6.4 g sugar, 3.2 g fiber • 226 mg sodium, 24 mg calcium, 1.7 mg iron, 20.9 mg vitamin C, 605 mcg beta-carotene, 0.7 mg vitamin E

CHANA PALAK
Rajput Indian Cuisine, Norfolk, Virginia

MAKES 2 SERVINGS

*C*hickpeas cooked in a mild gravy with spinach purée and tomato makes for a healthy and hearty meal.

1 teaspoon cumin seeds
1 teaspoon ginger-garlic paste (can substitute 1/2 teaspoon grated fresh ginger plus 1/2 teaspoon minced fresh garlic)
1/2 cup onion, chopped
4 tablespoons water, divided
1/4 cup tomato, chopped
1 teaspoon garam masala

1 teaspoon chana masala
1 teaspoon crushed fenugreek leaves, crushed by hand (optional)
1/2 cup canned chickpeas, drained
5 cups spinach, chopped
salt, to taste
1 teaspoon cilantro (coriander leaves), chopped

Heat a non-stick pan and add cumin seeds. Cook for 1 minute, then add ginger-garlic paste and sauté for 2 minutes. Add onion and 2 tablespoons water and cook over low-medium heat until light brown, then add tomato and continue cooking until mixture thickens. Add garam masala, chana masala, fenugreek leaves, and remaining 2 tablespoons water. Sauté for 2 to 3 minutes. Add chickpeas and mix well, then add spinach. Simmer, allowing mixture to thicken, for a few minutes. Add salt to taste. Garnish with cilantro.

Per serving (1/2 of recipe): 113 calories, 1.9 g fat, 0.2 g saturated fat, 15.2% calories from fat, 0 mg cholesterol • 6.7 g protein, 19.8 g carbohydrate, 2.8 g sugar, 5.3 g fiber • 256 mg sodium, 141 mg calcium, 5.3 mg iron, 13.1 mg vitamin C, 4042 mcg beta-carotene, 1.9 mg vitamin E

POTATO CAKES WITH CHICKPEA SALAD AND TAMARIND SAUCE
Mildreds, London, England

MAKES 4 SERVINGS

POTATO CAKES

1 pound new potatoes
1 tablespoon salt
2 tablespoons olive oil
1/2 tablespoon garlic, chopped
1 red chili, seeds removed, finely
    chopped

1 teaspoon ground nutmeg
2 tablespoons fresh cilantro,
    finely chopped
juice of 1/2 lemon
1 tablespoon chickpea flour or
    all-purpose flour

TAMARIND SAUCE

2 tablespoons vegetable oil
1/2 tablespoon garlic, chopped
1/4-inch piece fresh ginger, peeled
    and finely chopped
1 tablespoon cider vinegar

2 tablespoons superfine sugar
3 tablespoons soy sauce
1 1/2 tablespoons ketchup
1 tablespoon tamarind paste

CHICKPEA SALAD

3/4 cup cooked or canned chickpeas,
    drained

3/4 cup baby spinach leaves
2 green onions, finely sliced

For the potato cakes: Preheat oven to 350°F. Line a baking sheet with parchment paper and set aside. Place potatoes in a large saucepan of water, add salt, and bring to a boil. Cook until tender. Drain and set aside to cool. Heat oil in a small sauté pan, add garlic and chili, and cook 3 to 4 minutes, then remove from heat and set aside to cool. Crush cooled potatoes with your hands and mix in garlic-chili mixture, nutmeg, cilantro, lemon juice, and flour. Form into 8 balls and flatten. Place on prepared baking sheet and bake until crisp and golden, 30 to 45 minutes. Set aside.

For the tamarind sauce: Heat oil in a small pan over medium heat. Add garlic and ginger and sauté for 5 minutes. Add vinegar, sugar, soy sauce, ketchup, and tamarind paste. Cook for 10 minutes. Remove from heat and set aside.

For the chickpea salad: Toss chickpeas, spinach, and green onions together with half of the tamarind sauce, reserving the other half.

To serve, place warm potato cakes on top of chickpea salad and drizzle with remaining tamarind sauce.

Per serving (1/4 of recipe): 319 calories, 14.9 g fat, 2.3 g saturated fat, 41.1% calories from fat, 0 mg cholesterol • 6.5 g protein, 42.4 g carbohydrate, 10.2 g sugar, 5.7 g fiber • 1068 mg sodium, 63 mg calcium, 3.6 mg iron, 42.6 mg vitamin C, 485 mcg beta-carotene, 2 mg vitamin E

LINGUINE WITH PORTOBELLO MUSHROOM RAGU
VegiTerranean, Akron, Ohio

MAKES 4 SERVINGS

1 pound dry whole-wheat linguine
4 medium portobello mushrooms
6 tablespoons olive oil
2 medium sweet onions, finely chopped
2 teaspoons fresh garlic, minced
1 teaspoon fresh rosemary, finely chopped

salt, to taste
freshly ground black pepper, to taste
1 cup dry red wine, such as Chianti
1 28-ounce can chopped tomatoes, drained
grated vegan parmesan cheese, to taste

Cook pasta according to package directions. Drain and set aside.

Clean mushrooms, then remove and discard stems. Slice mushroom caps into 1/4-inch strips. Heat oil in a large skillet. Add onions and garlic and sauté over medium heat until translucent, about 5 minutes. Add mushrooms and cook, stirring occasionally, until they are quite tender and have begun to give off some liquid. Stir in rosemary, salt, and black pepper and cook for another 30 seconds. Add wine and simmer mushrooms until the liquid reduces by half, about 3 minutes. Add tomatoes and simmer until the sauce thickens, about 5 to 8 minutes. Taste and adjust salt and black pepper, if needed.

Toss the linguine with the mushroom sauce and divide among individual bowls. Serve immediately with grated vegan parmesan cheese.

Per serving (1/4 of recipe): 765 calories, 26.7 g fat, 3.8 g saturated fat, 30.6% calories from fat, 0 mg cholesterol • 27.8 g protein, 103.2 g carbohydrate, 8.1 g sugar, 12.8 g fiber • 644 mg sodium, 136 mg calcium, 5.9 mg iron, 15.7 mg vitamin C, 105 mcg beta-carotene, 5.1 mg vitamin E

ROASTED PORTOBELLO MUSHROOMS OVER SPELT BERRY AND BLACK BEAN SALAD WITH ORANGE-BASIL CREAM

Millennium Restaurant, San Francisco, California

MAKES 6 SERVINGS

ROASTED PORTOBELLO MUSHROOMS

6 portobello mushrooms, stems removed

1 tablespoon paprika (or chipotle chili powder if you like it spicy and smoky)

6 tablespoons soy sauce

1 teaspoon dried thyme

1/2 teaspoon black pepper

1 tablespoon brown sugar

SPELT BERRY AND BLACK BEAN SALAD

2 cups cooked, drained black beans

2 cups cooked whole spelt berries or brown rice

1 cup cherry tomatoes

1/2 red onion, finely chopped

1 garlic clove, finely chopped

1/2 cup fresh parsley, finely chopped

1/4 cup fresh mint, finely chopped

juice of 1 lemon

juice of 1 orange

salt to taste

ORANGE-BASIL CREAM

1/2 12.3-ounce package silken tofu

1 or 2 garlic cloves, minced

1/2 cup fresh basil leaves, blanched for 5 seconds and shocked in ice water

1 tablespoon nutritional yeast

juice of 1 orange

salt to taste

For the mushrooms: Preheat oven to 400°F. Place mushrooms cap side up on a sheet pan. Brush with soy sauce. Set aside. In a small bowl, combine paprika, thyme, black pepper, and sugar. Sprinkle over mushrooms. Roast mushrooms in a 400°F oven until they are cooked through and develop a nice crust on the cap. (Alternatively, seasoned mushrooms may be grilled.) Set cooked mushrooms aside.

For the salad: Combine black beans, spelt berries or rice, tomatoes, onion, garlic, parsley, mint, lemon juice, orange juice, and salt in a mixing bowl and toss together. Set aside.

For the cream: Place tofu, garlic, nutritional yeast, basil, orange juice, and salt in a food processor and blend until smooth.

To serve, place a mound of the salad toward the back of a dinner plate. Slice each mushroom into 4 to 6 slices and fan on top of the salad. Drizzle orange-basil cream on top of mushrooms and around the plates.

Per serving (1/6 of recipe): 249 calories, 2.6 g fat, 0.4 g saturated fat, 8.9% calories from fat, 0 mg cholesterol • 15.5 g protein, 45.3 g carbohydrate, 7.4 g sugar, 12 g fiber • 1442 mg sodium, 98 mg calcium, 4.9 mg iron, 26.6 mg vitamin C, 826 mcg beta-carotene, 1.1 mg vitamin E

PASTA AND VEGGIES WITH ALFREDO SAUCE

Lovin' Spoonfuls, Tucson, Arizona

MAKES 4 SERVINGS

PASTA
12 ounces dry whole-wheat linguine

VEGETABLES

1 tablespoon olive oil	1 red bell pepper, chopped
1/2 onion, coarsely chopped	3 carrots, thinly sliced
1/2 cup water	1 cup fresh or frozen green peas
1 cup broccoli florets	

ALFREDO SAUCE

2 tablespoons nutritional yeast	1/4 teaspoon dried oregano
2 tablespoons all-purpose flour	dash white pepper
1 teaspoon dried parsley	2 1/4 cups soymilk, divided
1 1/2 teaspoons garlic salt	1 tablespoon vegan margarine
1 teaspoon garlic powder	

For the pasta: Cook pasta according to package directions. Drain and set aside.

For the vegetables: Heat oil in a large sauté pan over medium heat. Add onion and sauté until tender. Add water, broccoli, bell pepper, carrots, and peas. Sauté until vegetables are tender and the water has evaporated. Add to cooked pasta and set aside.

For the Alfredo sauce: Blend nutritional yeast, flour, parsley, garlic salt and powder, oregano, white pepper, and 1/4 cup soymilk into a smooth paste. Place mixture in a saucepan and slowly dilute the paste while stirring in the remaining 2 cups soymilk. Bring the sauce to just boiling. Blend in margarine.

Toss sauce with pasta and vegetables and serve.

Per serving (1/4 of recipe): 534 calories, 10.4 g fat, 1.7 g saturated fat, 16.9% calories from fat, 0 mg cholesterol • 23.9 g protein, 94.2 g carbohydrate, 11.8 g sugar, 14 g fiber • 520 mg sodium, 251 mg calcium, 5.6 mg iron, 68.2 mg vitamin C, 4293 mcg beta-carotene, 4.6 mg vitamin E

PENNE WITH BROCCOLI RAAB

Navedano, Como, Italy

MAKES 6 SERVINGS

2 tablespoons extra-virgin olive oil
2 garlic cloves
1 hot pepper, finely chopped, or to taste
8 ounces dry penne pasta

2 1/2 cups broccoli raab (washed and
    stems removed)
3/4 cup halved cherry tomatoes
salt, to taste

Bring a medium pot of water to a boil.

Meanwhile, heat oil in a separate small frying pan and sauté garlic and hot pepper for a few minutes. Set frying pan aside.

Add broccoli raab to the boiling water for 30 seconds, then remove broccoli raab with a strainer or slotted spoon and set aside. Add pasta to water, cooking it according to the package directions.

Add broccoli raab and tomatoes to the frying pan with the garlic and hot pepper and sauté for 4 minutes. Add salt to taste. Drain pasta, toss with sautéed vegetables, and serve.

Per serving (1/6 of recipe): 215 calories, 5.6 g fat, 0.8 g saturated fat, 22.7% calories from fat, 0 mg cholesterol • 6.9 g protein, 34.3 g carbohydrate, 1.5 g sugar, 2.6 g fiber • 157 mg sodium, 30 mg calcium, 1.9 mg iron, 21.6 mg vitamin C, 362 mcg beta-carotene, 1.1 mg vitamin E

SPIRAL CHILI

Spiral Diner & Bakery, Fort Worth, Texas

MAKES 8 SERVINGS

*W*ith a motto of "Vegans get plenty," Spiral Diner & Bakery is a delight for the senses.

2 tablespoons vegetable oil
1 white or red onion, chopped
5 garlic cloves, chopped
1 28-ounce can crushed tomatoes

1 tablespoon dried oregano
1/2 cup vegetable broth
1 15-ounce can black beans, drained
    and rinsed

1 1/2 cups dry texturized vegetable protein (TVP)
1 cup water
2 tablespoons ground cumin
1 1/2 teaspoons sea salt

1 15-ounce can kidney beans, drained and rinsed
1/4 cup vegan sour cream, for garnish
1/4 cup chives, chopped, for garnish

In a large soup pot, heat oil over medium-high heat. Add onion and garlic and sauté until soft and translucent. Stir in tomatoes, TVP, water, cumin, salt, oregano, broth, and beans. Bring mixture to a boil. Lower heat and simmer for about 10 minutes, adding more water if necessary. Serve chili topped with sour cream and chives.

Per serving (1/8 of recipe): 233 calories, 5.9 g fat, 2 g saturated fat, 22.4% calories from fat, 0 mg cholesterol • 16.5 g protein, 30.7 g carbohydrate, 5.5 g sugar, 10.2 g fiber • 769 mg sodium, 144 mg calcium, 5.7 mg iron, 12.4 mg vitamin C, 155 mcg beta-carotene, 1.2 mg vitamin E

CURRY TOFU STIR-FRY

Pun Pun, Mae Taeng, Thailand

MAKES 3 SERVINGS

*T*his dish is great served over rice.

1/4 cup reduced-sodium soy sauce
4 teaspoons sugar
4 teaspoons yellow curry powder
2 cups mushrooms, sliced
2 large carrots, grated
4 green onions, cut into 1-inch pieces

3 celery stalks, cut into 1-inch pieces
1 cup baby corn, sliced
chili paste, to taste
2 tablespoons olive oil
16 ounces firm tofu, cut into 1 1/2-inch cubes

In a medium bowl, mix soy sauce, sugar, and curry powder. Add mushrooms, carrots, green onions, celery, baby corn, and chili paste and toss to cover. Set aside.

Heat oil in a wok. Add tofu and fry until golden brown and crispy on the outside.

Pour vegetable mixture over tofu in wok and stir-fry quickly until vegetables are cooked, about 10 minutes. Remove from heat and serve.

Per serving (1/3 of recipe): 307 calories, 16.5 g fat, 2.8 g saturated fat, 46.4% calories from fat, 0 mg cholesterol • 17 g protein, 29.7 g carbohydrate, 11.3 g sugar, 6.6 g fiber • 992 mg sodium, 365 mg calcium, 5.1 mg iron, 13.4 mg vitamin C, 3908 mcg beta-carotene, 2.6 mg vitamin E

Chausson d'Epinards
Le Ponant

Le Ponant is a French luxury yacht that lands at ports of call from the Mediterranean to the Indian Ocean. On April 4, 2008, *Le Ponant* was captured by Somali pirates and held for ransom. After eight days of tense negotiations, the boat and crew were released. Immediately thereafter, French helicopters came out of the sky, chasing the pirates into the desert. French commandos captured six of them, bringing them France for trial. Meanwhile, the crew of *Le Ponant* didn't miss a beat, and jumped right back into service. Today, the boat is safe, secure, and friendly as ever, and its restaurant serves up this savory dish, reminiscent of spanakopita.

3 tablespoons olive oil, divided
3 garlic cloves, minced
1 onion, chopped
1 teaspoon salt, divided
1 1/2 pounds fresh spinach

1/2 teaspoon ground nutmeg
8 sheets vegan phyllo dough, thawed
3 small tomatoes (about 3/4 pound),
 cored

Heat 1 1/2 tablespoons oil in a sauté pan over medium heat. Add garlic and cook until browned, about 3 minutes. Add onion and 1/2 teaspoon salt. Cook until tender. Add spinach, increase the heat to high, and sauté, stirring constantly, for about 3 minutes. Drain well. Add nutmeg, divide spinach filling in half, and wrap each half in 4 sheets phyllo dough. Add remaining 1 1/2 tablespoons oil to a clean sauté pan over medium-high heat and fry phyllo-spinach packets until phyllo is crunchy on the outside. Set aside.

Blend tomatoes and remaining 1/2 teaspoon salt in a food processor until smooth. Pour over phyllo-spinach packets and serve immediately.

Per serving (1/2 of recipe): 535 calories, 22 g fat, 3.2 g saturated fat, 36.2% calories from fat, 0 mg cholesterol • 14.9 g protein, 73.5 g carbohydrate, 8 g sugar, 9.5 g fiber • 1627 mg sodium, 327 mg calcium, 11.1 mg iron, 41.6 mg vitamin C, 13705 mcg beta-carotene, 8 mg vitamin

PASULJ PREBRANAC
Restaurant Roma, Budva, Montenegro

MAKES 6 SERVINGS

*T*his tiny restaurant on Montenegro's coast features this hearty traditional bean dish.

3 cups cooked large white beans
water
3 bay leaves
1/4 cup olive oil
2 cups onions, coarsely chopped

1 tablespoon paprika
1 tablespoon salt
2 large carrots, sliced
1 1/2 teaspoons black pepper

Preheat oven to 400°F.

Place beans in a medium pot, cover beans with water, add bay leaves, and bring to a boil over high heat. Boil for about 10 minutes. Drain and set aside. Meanwhile, in another medium pan, heat oil over medium heat. Add onions and sauté until golden brown. Add paprika and salt, mix well, and cook for 30 seconds, then remove from heat. Add carrots, then combine mixture with beans. Add desired amount of water to taste, at least 1 to 2 cups (after it is baked, *pasulj prebranac* can be completely dry or have the texture of a thick sauce, depending on the amount of water added). Transfer beans to a casserole dish and bake for 20 minutes or until the top browns.

Per serving (1/6 of recipe): 235 calories, 9.6 g fat, 1.4 g saturated fat, 36% calories from fat, 0 mg cholesterol • 9.6 g protein, 29.6 g carbohydrate, 3.5 g sugar, 7.4 g fiber • 1468 mg sodium, 103 mg calcium, 3.9 mg iron, 4.1 mg vitamin C, 2153 mcg beta-carotene, 2.7 mg vitamin E

ORECCHIETTE WITH BRAISED VEGETABLES

Sublime, Fort Lauderdale, Florida

MAKES 10 TO 12 SERVINGS

1 pound fennel
1/4 cup vegan margarine, divided
3 or 4 garlic cloves, divided
1 teaspoon dried thyme
Kosher salt, to taste
1 1/2 cups dry white wine, such as Chardonnay, divided
3 cups vegetable broth, divided
1 1/2 cups extra-virgin olive oil
3 cups cherry tomatoes
1 pound zucchini
2 pounds dry orecchiette pasta
1/4 cup fresh garlic, chopped
1 pound fresh fava beans or lima beans

Braise the fennel: Trim the stalks off the fennel and cut each bulb lengthwise into quarters. In a large saucepan, melt 2 tablespoons margarine over medium heat. Add fennel, 2 garlic cloves, and thyme, and toss the fennel to coat it with margarine. Add salt to taste. Add 1/2 cup of the wine and 2 cups of the vegetable broth. If this doesn't cover the fennel, add a little water. Bring the mixture to a boil, reduce it to a simmer, and then cover. Braise the fennel for 15 to 20 minutes. Remove fennel. Save the chardonnay/vegetable broth mixture.

Poach the cherry tomatoes: In a medium sauté pan, add oil (about half an inch). Heat oil until it is just below frying temperature. Season the oil with salt and 1 or 2 garlic cloves, cut in half. Carefully add tomatoes (oil should just barely cover them) and poach until they swell up and almost burst, about 3 to 4 minutes. Remove tomatoes. Save the oil mixture.

Grill the zucchini: Cut the zucchini lengthwise into long, thin strips. Coat the strips in some of the oil used to poach the tomatoes, and place on a hot grill. Grill them until they are brown, then flip them over and brown the other side.

Cook pasta according to package directions. Drain and set it aside.

Heat a heavy bottom stockpot on high. Heat about 1/2 cup of the olive oil (from poaching cherry tomatoes) and add the chopped garlic. Cook for about 30 seconds. Add fava beans, fennel, tomatoes, and zucchini and warm through. Add the remaining 1 cup wine and cook until it nearly evaporates. Add about half of the vegetable broth mixture (from braising the fennel) and do the same. Add the remaining 2 tablespoons margarine and swirl it through the vegetables. Toss the pasta with the sauce and divide into serving bowls. Serve immediately or reheat at a later time.

Per serving (1/10 of recipe): 610 calories, 18.6 g fat, 3 g saturated fat, 26.8% calories from fat, 0 mg cholesterol • 18 g protein, 89.5 g carbohydrate, 4.8 g sugar, 8.1 g fiber • 301 mg sodium, 64 mg calcium, 4.8 mg iron, 25.7 mg vitamin C, 554 mcg beta-carotene, 2.4 mg vitamin E

MOROCCAN-SPICED CHICKPEA CAKES
Candle 79, New York, New York

MAKES 6 SERVINGS

CHICKPEA CAKES

1/4 cup extra-virgin olive oil
1/2 cup onion, chopped
1/2 cup celery, chopped
3 cups cooked chickpeas
1 tablespoon sea salt

1 tablespoon Old Bay seasoning
1 teaspoon ground cumin
1 teaspoon paprika
2 tablespoons fresh parsley, chopped

RED PEPPER CURRY SAUCE

1/4 cup grapeseed oil
1 white onion, chopped
3 roasted red peppers, peeled and
   seeded
1 cup light coconut milk

1 teaspoon curry powder
1 teaspoon ground cumin
1 teaspoon sea salt
1/4 cup fresh cilantro, chopped
3 tablespoons tomato paste

MIXED VEGETABLES

2 tablespoons extra-virgin olive oil
1 cup white onion, chopped
1 cup Yukon gold potatoes, finely
    chopped, boiled until tender

1 cup fresh corn kernels
1 cup zucchini, chopped
1 teaspoon salt
1 tablespoon fresh parsley, chopped

APRICOT CHUTNEY

2 tablespoons grapeseed oil
1 cup white onions, chopped
3 cups fresh apricots, chopped
1/4 teaspoon salt

2 tablespoons agave nectar
2 tablespoons fresh ginger, grated
1/2 cup water

TOASTED ALMONDS

1/2 cup raw almonds

For the chickpea cakes: Heat oil in a medium saucepan over medium heat. Add onion and celery and sauté until tender. Remove to a medium bowl and set aside. Place chickpeas in a food processor and process until ground. Add ground chickpeas, salt, Old Bay, cumin, paprika, and parsley to onion mixture. Stir to combine. Form mixture into palm-size cakes. Set aside.

For the red pepper curry sauce: Heat oil in a small saucepan over medium heat. Add onion and sauté until soft. Allow to cool. Place contents of saucepan, red peppers, coconut milk, curry powder, cumin, salt, cilantro, and tomato paste in a blender. Blend until smooth. Place mixture in a medium saucepan and cook over medium heat for 10 to 15 minutes. Set aside.

For the mixed vegetables: Heat oil in a large skillet. Add onion, potatoes, corn, and zucchini, and sauté until all vegetables are tender. Remove from heat and mix in salt and parsley. Set aside.

For the apricot chutney: Heat oil in a medium pan over medium heat. Add onions and sauté until soft. Add apricots, salt, agave nectar, ginger, and water and cook for 25 to 30 minutes over medium heat. Set aside.

For the toasted almonds: Preheat oven to $350°F$. Place almonds on a baking sheet in a single layer and toast in oven for 10 minutes. Set aside.

To assemble the dish: Top chickpea cakes with mixed vegetables, curry sauce, apricot chutney, and toasted almonds.

Per serving (1/6 of recipe): 634 calories, 38.9 g fat, 6.3 g saturated fat, 53.4% calories from fat, 0 mg cholesterol • 14.6 g protein, 64.4 g carbohydrate, 23.8 g sugar, 13.5 g fiber • 2474 mg sodium, 150 mg calcium, 5.7 mg iron, 120.8 mg vitamin C, 2253 mcg beta-carotene, 11.6 mg vitamin E

STUFFED SHIITAKE MUSHROOMS WITH MILLET AND KUDZU BEET SAUCE

Seed, Venice, California

MAKES 4 SERVINGS

MILLET

1/2 cup dry millet	pinch sea salt
1 1/2 cups water	

SAUCE

1/2 onion, chopped	1 tablespoon fresh oregano, chopped
1 3/4 cups plus 1 teaspoon water, divided	pinch sea salt
1 red beet, peeled and chopped	1 teaspoon kudzu powder
1 yellow beet, peeled and chopped	1/4 teaspoon umeboshi vinegar

STUFFED MUSHROOMS

2 tablespoons olive oil, divided	2 tablespoons fresh thyme
1/4 cup onion, chopped	pinch sea salt
1/4 cup carrot, chopped	12 fresh shiitake mushrooms with 2- to 3-inch caps, stems removed
1/4 cup celery, chopped	

For the millet: Pour millet into a mesh strainer. Place strainer in a bowl under cold running water and rinse until water is clear, usually three times or more. Drain thoroughly. Transfer millet to a medium saucepan. Over medium heat, toast the grains, stirring frequently, until dry. Add water and salt. Bring to a boil, cover, and simmer for 20 minutes. Remove from heat, transfer to a large bowl, and allow to cool. Set aside.

For the sauce: In a saucepan, combine onion and 1/4 cup water. Sauté until onion becomes translucent. Add beets, oregano, salt, and 1 1/2 cups water. Bring to a boil, lower heat, and simmer until beets are tender, about 20 minutes. In a small bowl, dissolve kudzu powder in 1 teaspoon water. Add kudzu mixture and vinegar to

pan and simmer for 2 minutes more. Transfer to a blender and purée until smooth. Set aside until ready to use.

For the stuffed mushrooms: Heat 1 tablespoon oil in a wide saucepan over medium heat. Add onion, carrot, and celery and sauté for 2 minutes. Add thyme and salt and continue cooking for another minute. Transfer mixture to the bowl of millet and stir well to combine. Divide the millet mixture evenly among the mushrooms while it is still warm. Warm remaining I tablespoon oil and pan-fry stuffed mushrooms, millet side down first, for a few minutes on each side. Serve warm with sauce on the side.

Per serving (1/4 of recipe): 213 calories, 8.1 g fat, 1.2 g saturated fat, 33.2% calories from fat, 0 mg cholesterol • 4.5 g protein, 32.6 g carbohydrate, 4.1 g sugar, 4.7 g fiber • 263 mg sodium, 34 mg calcium, 1.7 mg iron, 4.8 mg vitamin C, 690 mcg beta-carotene, 1.2 mg vitamin E

Vegetables and Grains

GARDEN VEGETABLE TERRINE
WITH BASIL PESTO
AND TOMATO VINAIGRETTE

Navedano, Como, Italy

MAKES 6 SERVINGS

VEGETABLES

3/4 pound zucchini, thinly sliced
3/4 pound eggplant, thinly sliced
3/4 pound carrots, thinly sliced

3/4 pound bell peppers, thinly sliced
3/4 pound asparagus, bottoms
    snapped off

BASIL PESTO

1 1/2 cups fresh basil leaves (loosely
    packed)
1/2 cup extra-virgin olive oil

1 1/2 teaspoons salt
1/4 cup pine nuts

TOMATO VINAIGRETTE

1/2 cup red onion, chopped
1/4 cup balsamic vinegar
1/2 cup fresh tomatoes, chopped

1/4 cup extra-virgin olive oil
1/2 teaspoon orange zest
1/2 teaspoon lemon zest

For the vegetables: Steam zucchini, eggplant, carrots, bell peppers, and asparagus until tender. Set aside.

For the pesto: Place basil, oil, salt, and pine nuts in a food processor and blend well. Set aside.

For the vinaigrette: Place a small saucepan over medium heat. Add onion and balsamic vinegar and cook for 10 minutes. Remove from heat, then stir in tomatoes, oil, orange zest, and lemon zest. Set aside.

Layer vegetables into a mold, such as a medium plastic container, alternating vegetables with pesto. Cover top of terrine with plastic wrap, stack heavy cans on top, and let terrine rest in the refrigerator until thoroughly chilled, about 2 hours. Remove terrine from refrigerator, slice, and serve with prepared vinaigrette on the side.

Per serving (1/6 of recipe): 353 calories, 31.4 g fat, 4.3 g saturated fat, 78% calories from fat, 0 mg cholesterol • 3.4 g protein, 17.9 g carbohydrate, 8.6 g sugar, 4.8 g fiber • 628 mg sodium, 52 mg calcium, 1.7 mg iron, 44.5 mg vitamin C, 4695 mcg beta-carotene, 5.3 mg vitamin E

ROTI OR CHAPATI

Rajput Indian Cuisine, Norfolk, Virginia

MAKES 12 TO 15 SERVINGS

5 cups whole-wheat flour
2 cups room-temperature water
1 1/2 cups whole-wheat flour on a large
    plate for dusting the dough before rolling

Place 5 cups flour in a large bowl. Make a well in the middle and pour in a stream of water in the center. Mix flour and water until dough is moist enough to be gathered into a rough mass. Continue mixing until the mixture cleans the sides of the bowl and has become a non-stick, kneadable dough. Rest the dough and cover it with moist cloth for 1 hour to relax and absorb the water.

Then, roll dough into balls into the size of a plum. Place remaining 1 1/2 cups flour on a large plate. Place a dough ball on floured plate and flatten with your hand. Remove from plate and roll the dough with rolling pin from center of dough. Turn dough a few times to make it round and thin, approximately 6 inches in diameter. Repeat with remaining dough balls.

To cook the roti/chapati, preheat a cast-iron skillet or a heavy base pan over medium heat and flip the rolled dough onto the skillet. When top bubbles appear, turn it over. When top bubbles appear on second side, remove bread from the skillet. Repeat this procedure for each piece of dough.

Per serving (1/12 of recipe): 203 calories, 1.1 g fat, 0.2 g saturated fat, 4.6% calories from fat, 0 mg cholesterol • 8.2 g protein, 43.5 g carbohydrate, 0.4 g sugar, 7.3 g fiber • 5 mg sodium, 22 mg calcium, 2.3 mg iron, 0 mg vitamin C, 3 mcg beta-carotene, 0.5 mg vitamin E

GOBI MATTAR MASALA

Rajput Indian Cuisine, Norfolk, Virginia

MAKES 4 SERVINGS

1 pound fresh cauliflower, chopped into bite-size pieces
2 teaspoons salt, plus more to taste
1 cup plus 6 tablespoons water, divided
1 teaspoon coriander seeds
1 teaspoon cumin seeds
6 bay leaves

2 teaspoons ginger-garlic paste
2 onions, finely chopped
1 medium tomato, finely chopped
1 teaspoon garam masala, plus more for garnish
1 cup frozen green peas
4 coriander leaves, for garnish

Combine cauliflower, salt, and 1 cup water in a pot and boil for 5 minutes. Drain and set aside.

Heat a non-stick sauté pan and add coriander seeds, cumin seeds, and bay leaves and dry sauté on low-medium heat for 1 minute. Add ginger-garlic paste and simmer for 2 minutes. Add onions and remaining 2 tablespoons water and sauté until translucent. Then add tomato and sauté for 1 minute. Add garam masala and salt to taste. Add cooked cauliflower, peas, and 4 tablespoons water and cook for 5 minutes. Before serving, garnish with a dash more of garam masala and coriander leaves.

Per serving (1/4 of recipe): 72 calories, 0.8 g fat, 0.1 g saturated fat, 9.9% calories from fat, 0 mg cholesterol • 4 g protein, 14.1 g carbohydrate, 5.4 g sugar, 3.7 g fiber • 370 mg sodium, 45 mg calcium, 1.7 mg iron, 39.2 mg vitamin C, 489 mcg beta-carotene, 0.3 mg vitamin E

FLOWERING COURGETTES WITH SAFFRON RISOTTO

Navedano, Como, Italy

MAKES 8 SERVINGS

6 1/2 cups vegetable broth
2 saffron threads
1/2 tablespoon saffron powder
2 tablespoons olive oil, divided
1 shallot, chopped
1 1/3 cups dry Arborio rice

1 cup zucchini (courgette), chopped
1/2 cup zucchini flowers
1/2 cup dry white wine
salt
black pepper

Place broth in a medium pot over medium heat.

Place saffron threads and saffron powder into a small cup and add a little hot broth to emulsify. Set aside.

Heat 1 tablespoon oil in a sauté pan over high heat. Add shallot and sauté for a few minutes. Add rice and zucchini (chopped, without flowers) and cook for a few minutes. Add wine and stir until liquid evaporates. Continue cooking over high heat, adding one ladle of broth at a time and allowing liquid to evaporate while stirring the rice mixture constantly. After adding the last ladleful of broth, add saffron broth, zucchini flowers, salt, black pepper, and remaining 1 tablespoon oil. Serve immediately.

Per serving (1/8 of recipe): 179 calories, 3.7 g fat, 0.5 g saturated fat, 18% calories from fat, 0 mg cholesterol • 2.8 g protein, 30.8 g carbohydrate, 2.7 g sugar, 0.7 g fiber • 914 mg sodium, 20 mg calcium, 1.4 mg iron, 1.7 mg vitamin C, 332 mcg beta-carotene, 0.6 mg vitamin E

WILD RICE SALAD
Ottolenghi, London, England

MAKES 5 SERVINGS

1 1/2 cups dry wild rice
1/2 cup roasted and shelled pistachios, coarsely chopped
1 1/4 cups dried apricots, soaked in hot water for 5 minutes, drained, and coarsely chopped
2 tablespoons fresh mint, coarsely chopped

3 cups packed arugula
2 green onions, coarsely chopped
juice of 2 lemons
zest of 1 lemon
2 tablespoons olive oil
1 large garlic clove, crushed
sea salt, to taste
freshly ground black pepper to taste

Place rice in a large pot and cover with water. Bring to a boil, then reduce heat and cook for 35 to 40 minutes, or until rice is cooked and some grains have started to split. Drain and rinse rice under cold water. In a bowl, mix rice, pistachios, and apricots. Add mint, arugula, green onions, lemon juice and zest, olive oil, garlic, salt, and pepper. Toss well and serve.

Per serving (1/5 of recipe): 398 calories, 12 g fat, 1.6 g saturated fat, 25.9% calories from fat, 0 mg cholesterol • 11.9 g protein, 66.6 g carbohydrate, 20.5 g sugar, 7.7 g fiber • 213 mg sodium, 70 mg calcium, 3.2 mg iron, 7.9 mg vitamin C, 958 mcg beta-carotene, 3.1 mg vitamin E

ℐesserts

TANGERINE CHIFFON CAKE WITH BLUEBERRY STEW
Seed, Venice, California

MAKES 12 SERVINGS

CAKE

1/4 cup olive oil

1 1/2 cups whole-wheat pastry flour

1 1/2 cups unbleached white flour

1 1/2 tablespoons aluminum-free baking powder

1/2 teaspoon sea salt

2 tablespoons poppy seeds

1/4 teaspoon turmeric

1/2 cup safflower oil

1 cup rice syrup or maple syrup

1 cup soymilk

zest of 1 tangerine

1/2 cup tangerine juice

1/2 cup tangerine sections

1 teaspoon vanilla extract

BLUEBERRY STEW

1/2 tablespoon kudzu powder

2 cups apple juice

2 cups fresh blueberries

SOY VANILLA CREAM

2 cups soymilk

1/2 vanilla bean

1/4 cup rice syrup

1 pinch sea salt

2 tablespoons kudzu powder

For the cake: Preheat oven to 350°F. Grease a 12-cup muffin pan with olive oil and set aside. In a large bowl, whisk together flours, baking powder, salt, poppy seeds, and turmeric. Set aside. In a separate bowl, whisk safflower oil, syrup, soymilk, tangerine zest, and tangerine juice until emulsified. Add wet mixture to dry mixture and whisk gently. Add tangerine sections. Stir to combine. Pour batter into muffin pan and bake for 25 minutes. Cakes are ready when a toothpick inserted in the center comes out clean. Allow cakes to cool for 10 minutes, then remove from pan. Place on a cooling rack and allow to cool completely.

For the blueberry stew: Dilute kudzu powder in apple juice in a small saucepan. Bring to a simmer. It will thicken after a few minutes.

Add blueberries and cook, stirring, for 3 minutes. Set aside.

For the soy vanilla cream: Place soymilk in a small saucepan over medium heat. Split vanilla bean lengthwise with a knife and add to soymilk. Bring mixture to a simmer. With a slotted spoon, remove vanilla bean. Scrape seeds from bean. Add seeds back into soymilk, discarding the rest of the bean. Add rice syrup and salt. In a separate small bowl, dissolve kudzu powder in 2 tablespoons water. Whisk kudzu mixture into soymilk mixture and cook for a few minutes. Transfer to a container and refrigerate until cool.

Serve blueberry stew over cakes with dollops of soy vanilla cream.

Per serving (1/12 of recipe): 420 calories, 15.9 g fat, 1.5 g saturated fat, 33.1% calories from fat, 0 mg cholesterol • 6.4 g protein, 67.3 g carbohydrate, 23.5 g sugar, 4.1 g fiber • 365 mg sodium, 220 mg calcium, 2.6 mg iron, 9.4 mg vitamin C, 26 mcg beta-carotene, 4.9 mg vitamin E

BROWN RICE PUDDING
Sublime, Fort Lauderdale, Florida

MAKES 8 SERVINGS

1/2 pound brown rice	1/2 cup raisins
1 1/2 cups soymilk	1/2 cup light brown sugar (tightly
1/2 cup golden raisins	packed)

ORANGE SAUCE

8 ounces vegan sour cream	1 cup fresh orange juice
1 teaspoon agave nectar	

Cook rice according to package directions. In a large pot, cover cooked rice with soymilk and add raisins and sugar. Cook, covered, over low heat until most of the soymilk has evaporated and the rice is creamy, about 1 hour.

In a separate bowl, whisk together vegan sour cream, agave nectar, and orange juice.

Divide rice pudding into serving bowls and serve slightly warm with orange sauce.

Per serving (1/8 of recipe): 311 calories, 7.3 g fat, 5.3 g saturated fat, 20.3% calories from fat, 0 mg cholesterol • 5.5 g protein, 58.4 g carbohydrate, 29.4 g sugar, 4.4 g fiber • 67 mg sodium, 92 mg calcium, 1.6 mg iron, 11.2 mg vitamin C, 9 mcg beta-carotene, 1 mg vitamin E

TARTES CHAUDES (AUX FRAMBOISES, AUX POMMES, AUX BANANES)

Pizzeria Bruno, Saint-Tropez, France

MAKES 8 SERVINGS

*G*o for the pizza—the best in the world—but stay for these delightful fruit tarts.

TARTES

1 recipe Pastry Dough (recipe follows)
1 recipe Vegan Crème Pâtissière (recipe follows)
3 cups raspberries, chopped apples, or sliced bananas

1/2 cup sugar
3 tablespoons rum, Calvados, or Grand Marnier (optional)
soy ice cream (optional)

PASTRY DOUGH

1/2 tablespoon active dry yeast
1/2 to 3/4 cup lukewarm water (105 to 115°F), divided

1 1/2 cups all-purpose flour
1/2 teaspoon salt
2 tablespoons olive oil, divided

In a small bowl, dissolve yeast in 1/4 cup lukewarm water. Let stand for 10 minutes or until frothy.

If mixing by hand: In a mixing bowl, mix flour and salt. Add dissolved yeast to dry ingredients with 1 tablespoon oil. Using a wooden spoon to mix, add just enough of the remaining 1/2 cup of lukewarm water to form the dough, adding a little more water if needed. Remove dough from the bowl to a floured pastry board. Knead for 8 to 10 minutes, or until dough is smooth and elastic. Lightly flour the board if the dough begins to stick. Form the dough into a ball.

If using a food processor: Combine flour and salt in a food processor fitted with a metal blade. With the motor running, gradually pour dissolved yeast and oil through the feed tube and add just enough of the remaining 1/2 cup of lukewarm water until the dough forms a ball. Let the dough spin for 30 to 60 seconds, or until smooth and elastic.

Transfer dough ball to a bowl coated with remaining 1 tablespoon oil. Cover with a damp towel or plastic wrap and let rise in a warm, draft-free place for 1 hour or until the dough has doubled in bulk. (You may prepare the filling while the dough is rising.)

When the dough has doubled in bulk, punch it down and knead it for 15 seconds. Let the dough rest under a towel for 10 minutes before proceeding with the recipe. If you are not ready to the bake after punching the dough down, set the covered bowl in a cooler place, where it will keep safely for an hour or more. You can chill or even freeze the dough, but remember to leave enough time to bring it back to room temperature so the dough can start to rise again before you form a crust and bake it.

VEGAN CRÈME PÂTISSIÈRE

1/4 cup unbleached flour	2 tablespoons lemon juice
1 cup soymilk, divided	1 teaspoon grated lemon zest
1/4 cup sugar	1/2 teaspoon vanilla extract
pinch of salt	

Place flour in a small bowl. Whisk in 1/4 cup soymilk and set aside.

In a small saucepan, whisk together the remaining 3/4 cup soymilk, sugar, and salt. Add the flour mixture and whisk well to combine. Cook the mixture over medium heat, while whisking constantly, for 5 to 6 minutes, or until thickened. Add lemon juice, lemon zest, and vanilla. Whisk well to combine, and cook the mixture 1 additional minute. Remove the saucepan from the heat and transfer the mixture to a glass bowl.

Place a piece of wax paper or plastic wrap directly on top of the pastry cream to prevent a skin from forming on the top. Place the pastry cream in the refrigerator for several hours to cool completely before using.

Preheat oven to 375°F.

Roll and stretch out dough into a circle with a 10-inch diameter. Add crème pâtissière. Add fruit and sprinkle with sugar. Add a sprinkle of rum, Calvados, or Grand Marnier, if using (raspberries go well with Grand Marnier, bananas and apples go well with rum). Bake for about 20 minutes until dough is cooked, like a pizza. Top with soy ice cream, if using.

Per serving (1/8 of recipe, with raspberries): 246 calories, 4.5 g fat, 0.6 g saturated fat, 15.9% calories from fat, 0 mg cholesterol • 4.7 g protein, 47.9 g carbohydrate, 21.8 g sugar, 4.4 g fiber • 205 mg sodium, 55 mg calcium, 2 mg iron, 13.5 mg vitamin C, 6 mcg beta-carotene, 1.3 mg vitamin E

CHOCOLATE TRUFFLES
Seed, Venice, California

MAKES 24 TRUFFLES

TRUFFLES
1 cup soymilk
2 tablespoons agar flakes
18 ounces dairy-free, grain-sweetened chocolate chips
1 tablespoon cocoa powder

COATING
3/4 cup cocoa powder
OR 1 cup finely chopped roasted hazelnuts
OR 1 cup toasted coconut flakes

In a saucepan over medium heat, bring soymilk and agar to a simmer, stirring until agar flakes are completely dissolved. Add cocoa powder and chocolate chips and stir well until melted.

Remove from heat and transfer mixture to a baking pan. Allow to cool, then refrigerate for 1 hour.

Using a spoon, scoop up about 2 tablespoons of the chocolate mixture. Roll between your hands to form a small ball. Continue until mixture is used up.

Roll each ball in the cocoa powder, chopped hazelnuts, or coconut flakes.

Store in the refrigerator until ready to serve.

Per truffle (with cocoa powder coating): 114 calories, 6.9 g fat, 4 g saturated fat, 51.6% calories from fat, 0 mg cholesterol • 1.8 g protein, 15.7 g carbohydrate, 11.6 g sugar, 2.4 g fiber • 9 mg sodium, 23 mg calcium, 1.2 mg iron, 0 mg vitamin C, 15 mcg beta-carotene, 0.2 mg vitamin E

COCONUT, LEMON, TOFU, AND MAPLE SYRUP CHEESECAKE

Mildreds, London, England

MAKES 8 SERVINGS

14 ounces firm tofu
7 ounces crushed graham cracker crumbs
1/2 cup vegan margarine, slightly softened but not melted
3 bananas, thinly sliced

7 ounces coconut milk
7 ounces maple syrup
1/4 cup sugar
juice and zest of 2 lemons
1 1/2 tablespoons agar flakes

Mix graham cracker crumbs and margarine together and press into base of a 10-inch springform pan. Place bananas on top of base and refrigerate until ready to fill.

Place tofu and coconut milk in a blender and process until completely smooth. Set aside.

Place maple syrup, sugar, and lemon juice and zest in a small pot over high heat. Cook for 5 minutes until sugar has dissolved. Reduce heat to low, add agar flakes and cook for another 10 minutes or until agar has completely dissolved.

Add maple syrup mixture to tofu mixure and blend well. Pour over graham cracker base. Chill in refrigerator until firm, at least 2 hours.

Per serving (1/8 of cheesecake): 422 calories, 21.3 g fat, 7.9 g saturated fat, 43.8% calories from fat, 0 mg cholesterol • 7.1 g protein, 55.2 g carbohydrate, 34.4 g sugar, 3.1 g fiber • 301 mg sodium, 148 mg calcium, 2.2 mg iron, 7.1 mg vitamin C, 114 mcg beta-carotene, 0.7 mg vitamin E

APPLE PIE

Spiral Diner & Bakery, Fort Worth, Texas

MAKES 2 PIES

HOMEMADE PIE CRUST (MAKES 2 CRUSTS)

3 cups unbleached white flour, plus more if needed
2 tablespoons powdered sugar
1 1/4 teaspoons sea salt
1 1/4 teaspoons baking powder

1/2 cup chilled vegetable shortening
2/3 cup chilled vegan margarine
6 tablespoons ice-cold water
2 teaspoons apple cider vinegar

APPLE PIE FILLING

8 medium apples, peeled, cored, and sliced into thin lengthwise pieces
1 cup sugar
4 teaspoons tapioca starch
1 1/2 teaspoons ground cinnamon

1/4 teaspoon sea salt
1 tablespoon lemon juice
2 tablespoons agave nectar or maple syrup

APPLE PIE TOPPING

2/3 cup flour
2/3 cup sugar
2 tablespoons plus 1 teaspoon ground cinnamon

1/2 teaspoon sea salt
1/2 teaspoon ground nutmeg
1/4 cup vegan margarine

For the pie crust: In a medium mixing bowl, whisk together flour, sugar, salt, and baking powder. Divide shortening and margarine into tablespoon-size chunks and, using a pastry blender or two knives, cut them into flour mixture. Mix until shortening and margarine are roughly blended. Combine water and vinegar in a small bowl and add to flour mixture. Mix until a dough ball forms. If dough is too sticky, add a few more tablespoons flour and continue mixing. Cover dough with plastic wrap and chill for at least 20 minutes.

After 20 minutes, separate dough into two even balls (about 1 1/4 cups each). Keep dough refrigerated until ready to assemble the pie. The dough can also be frozen for later use.

To roll out dough, flatten it into a disk and place it between two 12-inch pieces of parchment. Roll it out into a circle to fit a 9-inch pie pan. Peel off the top layer of parchment, place a pie dish evenly on top of the dough and flip it over. Then peel the paper off and crimp the edges with a fork for decoration. Repeat with remaining dough ball.

For the filling: Place apples in a large mixing bowl. In a separate medium mixing bowl, whisk together sugar, tapioca, starch, cinnamon, and salt. Add sugar mixture, lemon juice, and agave nectar or maple syrup to apples. Mix well, covering all of the apples evenly.

Divide apple pie filling evenly between the two 9-inch pie shells.

For the topping: Place flour, sugar, salt, cinnamon, nutmeg, and margarine in a medium mixing bowl. Using a pastry blender or two knives, cut all ingredients together. The mix should be crumbly. Do not overmix. Crumble topping evenly over pies. Leave a few tiny holes for steam to escape.

When ready to bake, preheat oven to 350°F. Place prepared pies in preheated oven and bake for about one hour. The pies are done when the crust is brown and thick bubbles are coming out of the holes, which means the tapioca has activated.

Per serving (1/8 of 1 pie): 392 calories, 17.3 g fat, 3.9 g saturated fat, 39% calories from fat, 0 mg cholesterol • 3.4 g protein, 57.9 g carbohydrate, 31.6 g sugar, 2.7 g fiber • 455 mg sodium, 54 mg calcium, 1.7 mg iron, 3.5 mg vitamin C, 78 mcg beta-carotene, 0.5 mg vitamin E

ESPRESSO BROWNIES

Horizons, Philadelphia, Pennsylvania

MAKES 12 SERVINGS

BROWNIES

3 cups flour	2 3/4 cups vegan chocolate chips
2 cups sugar	6 tablespoons vegetable shortening
1 1/2 teaspoons baking powder	2 tablespoons instant coffee
1/2 cup vegan margarine	2 cups soymilk

ICING

3 cups powdered sugar	1 teaspoon vanilla extract
1/4 cup vegan margarine, softened	1/4 cup cold coffee or espresso

cocoa powder, powdered sugar, coffee beans, or melted chocolate for garnish (optional)

For the brownies: Preheat oven to 350°F. Line a baking pan with parchment paper (or coat with margarine and a light dusting of flour). In a large mixing bowl, combine flour, sugar, and baking powder and set aside. In a separate medium saucepan over low heat, melt margarine, then add chocolate chips and melt. Add shortening and instant coffee, stirring with a spoon until very smooth, then add soymilk. Remove chocolate mixture from heat and allow to cool for a few minutes. Add melted ingredients to dry ingredients, and stir quickly until combined. Pour batter into prepared pan and bake for 30 minutes or until a fork comes out clean, rotating halfway through to ensure even baking. Remove brownies from oven and allow to cool thoroughly (about 1 1/2 hours) before icing.

For the icing: While the brownies are baking, combine powdered sugar, margarine, vanilla, and coffee or espresso in a food processor and blend until smooth. Refrigerate until needed.

If desired, garnish iced brownies with cocoa powder, powdered sugar, coffee beans, or melted chocolate.

Per serving (1/12 of recipe): 727 calories, 30.4 g fat, 11 g saturated fat, 36.3% calories from fat, 0 mg cholesterol • 6.5 g protein, 114.9 g carbohydrate, 84 g sugar, 3.8 g fiber • 224 mg sodium, 107 mg calcium, 3.2 mg iron, 0.2 mg vitamin C, 69 mcg beta-carotene, 1.2 mg vitamin E

Breakfasts

BLACK SESAME BISCOTTI OR
ALMOND ANISE BISCOTTI
Seed, Venice, California

MAKES 24 BISCOTTI

1 1/2 cups pastry flour
1 1/2 cups unbleached all-purpose flour
1/2 tablespoon aluminum-free baking powder
3/8 teaspoon sea salt
1/3 cup maple sugar
1/2 cup black sesame seeds (for Black Sesame Biscotti)

Or 2 cups whole dry-roasted unsalted almonds plus 2 tablespoons anise seeds (for Almond Anise Biscotti)
2/3 cup soymilk
1 1/2 teaspoons kudzu powder
1/3 cup maple syrup or rice syrup
1/4 cup safflower oil
2 teaspoons vanilla extract
2 teaspoons lemon juice

Preheat oven to 325°F.

In a large bowl, combine flours, baking powder, salt, and maple sugar. Add black sesame seeds or almonds and anise seeds. In a separate bowl, whisk together soymilk, kudzu powder, syrup, oil, vanilla, and lemon juice until emulsified. Add wet mixture to dry mixture and combine well by hand.

Separate dough into 2 halves. Using your hands, form 2 logs, each about 4 inches by 10 inches. Press each log down firmly so that the bottom side of the biscotti will be flat. Pull in both sides of the dough log with your hands so that the edges do not become too thin.

Bake for 20 minutes. Cut each log into 12 slices and bake for another 15 minutes on each side. Cool and serve.

Per Black Sesame Biscotti: 127 calories, 4.5 g fat, 0.5 g saturated fat, 30.2% calories from fat, 0 mg cholesterol • 2.4 g protein, 19.6 g carbohydrate, 5.8 g sugar, 0.8 g fiber • 73 mg sodium, 33 mg calcium, 1.3 mg iron, 0.1 mg vitamin C, 1 mcg beta-carotene, 0.9 mg vitamin E

Per Almond Anise Biscotti: 176 calories, 8.3 g fat, 0.6 g saturated fat, 40.3% calories from fat, 0 mg cholesterol • 4.3 g protein, 22 g carbohydrate, 6.2 g sugar, 2 g fiber • 72 mg sodium, 65 mg calcium, 1.8 mg iron, 0.2 mg vitamin C, 1 mcg beta-carotene, 3.9 mg vitamin E

CILANTRO-LIME TOFU HASH
Bluegrass Grill and Bakery, Charlottesville, Virginia

MAKES 6 TO 8 SERVINGS

*C*harlottesville's Bluegrass Grill & Bakery is a fun and funky breakfast place with mismatched mugs, quilts, and bluegrass music. Be sure to leave yourself plenty of time for a leisurely breakfast in this cozy diner-like setting.

POTATOES
14 red rose or very small red-skinned potatoes

TOFU
2 16-ounce packages extra-firm tofu	1/2 teaspoon dried dill
1/4 teaspoon turmeric	1 1/2 teaspoons Spike Salt-Free
1/4 teaspoon granulated garlic	Magic seasoning
1/4 teaspoon granulated onion	3/4 teaspoon soy sauce

CILANTRO-LIME SAUCE

1 bunch fresh cilantro	1 tablespoon soy sauce
1/2 tablespoon olive oil	1/4 teaspoon sugar
1/2 cup lime juice	

HASH

2 tablespoons olive oil	1 tablespoon green onion, chopped
1/2 cup yellow onion, chopped	1 tablespoon green bell pepper,
2 teaspoons Spike Salt-Free Magic	chopped
seasoning	1/4 cup mushrooms, sliced
1/4 teaspoon black pepper	1/4 cup tomato, chopped
1/4 teaspoon onion powder	1 cup fresh spinach (packed)

Wash potatoes and place in a pot with enough water to just cover. Bring water to a strong boil, then lower heat to maintain a just-rolling boil for 15 to 20 minutes. Turn off heat and let the potatoes rest for 10 to 15 minutes—they are ready when a knife still meets a little resistance at their center. Pour off water, keeping potatoes in the pot, and fill the pot with cold water and ice cubes. After potatoes have cooled, drain and chop them into 1/2-inch chunks. Set aside.

Slice tofu into slabs. Fold paper towels or clean dish towels between slabs and press over sink to drain all excess water. In a medium bowl, crumble tofu and mix in turmeric, garlic, onion, dill, 1 1/2 teaspoons Spike seasoning, and 3/4 teaspoon soy sauce. Set aside.

Place cilantro, 1/2 tablespoon olive oil, lime juice, remaining 1 tablespoon soy sauce, and sugar in a food processor. Process until smooth. Set aside.

When ready to serve, heat oil in a large skillet over medium heat, then add potatoes and yellow onion, increasing the heat. Toss until onions soften, then add remaining 2 teaspoons Spike seasoning, black pepper, and onion powder. Fry for about 2 minutes, then add green onion, bell pepper, mushrooms, tomato, and spinach. After 2 more minutes, add tofu mixture. Cook and toss until tofu is heated uniformly. Add cilantro-lime sauce and cook for 1 minute longer, then serve.

Per serving (1/6 of recipe): 294 calories, 14.8 g fat, 1.7 g saturated fat, 43% calories from fat, 0 mg cholesterol • 17.7 g protein, 28 g carbohydrate, 3.1 g sugar, 4.3 g fiber • 216 mg sodium, 318 mg calcium, 5.6 mg iron, 24.6 mg vitamin C, 427 mcg beta-carotene, 1.2 mg vitamin E

TOFU BENEDICT

Horizons, Philadelphia, Pennsylvania

MAKES 3 SERVINGS

SAUCE

2 tablespoons vegan margarine
1/4 cup vegan mayonnaise
1 teaspoon Dijon mustard
salt, to taste

black pepper, to taste
1 teaspoon chopped fresh tarragon,
   thyme, or dill

OTHER INGREDIENTS

3 English muffins
3 teaspoons cayenne pepper
1 16-ounce block firm tofu, cut into 3
   equal slabs

4 tablespoons canola oil, divided
6 slices vegetarian bacon
1 very large ripe beefsteak or slicing
   tomato, cut into 3 thick slices

Sauce: Bring margarine to room temperature, letting it soften to the point that it is more melted than solid. In a mixing bowl, gently whisk together softened margarine, mayonnaise, mustard, salt, black pepper, and tarragon.

If sauce is too thick, drizzle in about 2 teaspoons cold water to thin it. If it breaks and liquefies, refrigerate immediately to thicken again. Set aside.

Slice English muffins, then toast them.

Rub cayenne pepper onto tofu and set aside. Heat 3 tablespoons oil in a skillet, add tofu, and pan-sear for 30 seconds on each side. Set aside.

In a separate sauté pan, heat the remaining 1 tablespoon oil over medium-high heat until it is gently rippling. Lightly fry vegetarian bacon for about 45 seconds on each side. Note: Do not overcook the bacon or it will get tough!

To serve, arrange a muffin half, bacon, tofu, and tomato on a serving plate. Place other muffin half on the side. Repeat with remaining plates. Drizzle sauce on top and serve immediately.

Per serving (1/3 of recipe): 516 calories, 33.6 g fat, 5.5 g saturated fat, 56.5% calories from fat, 0 mg cholesterol • 24.6 g protein, 34.9 g carbohydrate, 5.5 g sugar, 5.5 g fiber • 849 mg sodium, 521 mg calcium, 6.4 mg iron, 12.7 mg vitamin C, 790 mcg beta-carotene, 4.7 mg vitamin E

CIABATTA VEGETABLE BREAKFAST SCRAMBLE

Amalfi, Norfolk, Virginia

MAKES 6 SERVINGS

*A*malfi uses only the very best ingredients drawn from traditional Italian cuisine. From the start, chef Angelo always looked for ways to put healthfulness first, creating vegan versions of everything from calamari to chicken Boscaiola, chocolate gelato, and pistachio cheesecake. The scrumptious dishes are served to the sounds of Pavarotti and Dean Martin.

1/4 cup olive oil, divided
2 16-ounce packages firm tofu, pressed, drained, and crumbled
1/8 teaspoon turmeric
1/2 cup nutritional yeast
1/2 cup onion, chopped
2 red bell peppers, seeded and chopped

3 cups mushrooms, sliced
6 cups roughly chopped fresh spinach (packed)
2 14-ounce cans artichoke hearts in water, drained and cut into halves
1 cup grated vegan mozzarella
6 slices ciabatta bread, toasted

Heat 1 tablespoon oil in a large skillet over medium heat. Add tofu, turmeric, and nutritional yeast and stir. Set aside. In a separate medium skillet, heat remaining 3 tablespoons oil over medium heat. Add onion and cook until tender. Add bell peppers and mushrooms, stirring and cooking until tender. Add spinach and artichoke hearts, cooking until spinach has wilted. Add vegetables to tofu mixture, stir, then sprinkle with vegan mozzarella. Serve with ciabatta toast.

Per serving (1/6 of recipe): 406 calories, 19.5 g fat, 3.6 g saturated fat, 41.6% calories from fat, 0 mg cholesterol • 26.8 g protein, 39 g carbohydrate, 9.1 g sugar, 14.2 g fiber • 519 mg sodium, 503 mg calcium, 5.8 mg iron, 76 mg vitamin C, 2171 mcg beta-carotene, 2.7 mg vitamin E

FRENCH TOAST
Amalfi, Norfolk, Virginia

MAKES 4 SERVINGS

2 cups vanilla soymilk
1/2 cup sugar
1/4 cup maple syrup
1/2 teaspoon salt
1/8 teaspoon ground nutmeg

1/8 teaspoon ground cinnamon
8 slices whole-wheat bread
non-stick cooking spray
2 bananas, sliced
2 cups sliced strawberries

Combine soymilk, sugar, maple syrup, salt, nutmeg, and cinnamon in a blender. Blend until smooth. Pour into a flat dish.

Coat a non-stick skillet with cooking spray and place over medium-high heat. Dip bread slices in batter, soaking until soft but not soggy. Cook each slice over medium-high heat for about 3 minutes on each side, until golden brown. Serve with bananas and strawberries.

Per serving (1/4 of recipe): 447 calories, 4.4 g fat, 0.8 g saturated fat, 8.5% calories from fat, 0 mg cholesterol • 13 g protein, 92.9 g carbohydrate, 58.6 g sugar, 8.4 g fiber • 636 mg sodium, 242 mg calcium, 3.4 mg iron, 54.3 mg vitamin C, 24 mcg beta-carotene, 2.3 mg vitamin E

BLUEBERRY MAPLE-PECAN SPICE MUFFINS
Greens, San Francisco, California

MAKES 10 MUFFINS

canola oil spray
1 cup all-purpose flour
1 cup cake flour
3 tablespoons maple sugar or brown
    sugar
1 teaspoon baking powder
1/2 teaspoon ground allspice
1/4 teaspoon ground ginger
1/4 teaspoon ground cardamom
1/4 teaspoon salt

3/4 cup vanilla soymilk
3/4 cup and 2 tablespoons maple
    syrup
1/4 cup canola oil
2 tablespoons pure vanilla extract
1 tablespoon unfiltered apple cider
    vinegar
1 pint fresh blueberries
1 recipe Maple-Pecan Streusel

MAPLE-PECAN STREUSEL (MAKES ABOUT 3/4 CUP)

1/2 cup pecan pieces, toasted and finely
    chopped (about 2 ounces)
1/4 cup maple sugar
1 1/2 tablespoons canola oil

Combine pecans, maple sugar, and canola oil in a small bowl and use your fingertips to mix them together.

Preheat oven to 350°F and set oven racks to the middle and top positions. Coat muffin tins with canola oil spray.

Sift flours, sugar, baking powder, allspice, ginger, cardamom, and salt together in a large bowl. In a separate bowl, whisk soymilk, maple syrup, canola oil, vanilla, and vinegar together and gently fold into dry ingredients until just mixed, being careful not to overwork the batter. Gently fold blueberries into batter. Divide batter into muffin tins, filling them 2/3 full. Sprinkle about 1 tablespoon streusel on each muffin. Bake on middle rack for 15 minutes. Rotate the pan, move to the top rack, and bake until muffins are golden and the center springs back to the touch, about 10 minutes more. Allow muffins to cool in the pan for about 10 minutes, then transfer to a cooling rack.

Tip: If you don't have cake flour, just use another cup of all-purpose flour. The muffins won't be as light, but they'll still be delicious.

Per muffin: 334 calories, 12.1 g fat, 1 g saturated fat, 31.5% calories from fat, 0 mg cholesterol • 3.8 g protein, 52.7 g carbohydrate, 27.2 g sugar, 2.1 g fiber • 124 mg sodium, 84 mg calcium, 2.5 mg iron, 3 mg vitamin C, 12 mcg beta-carotene, 1.8 mg vitamin E

PANCAKES

Spiral Diner & Bakery, Fort Worth, Texas

MAKES 8 SERVINGS

3 cups all-purpose flour
1/2 cup whole-wheat pastry flour
1/4 cup sugar
1 1/2 tablespoons baking powder
1 1/4 teaspoons salt
1 teaspoon ground ginger
1 teaspoon ground cinnamon

3 3/4 cups soymilk
1/2 cup sunflower oil
4 teaspoons vanilla extract
4 teaspoons almond extract
non-stick cooking spray
1/4 cup vegan margarine for serving
1 cup pure maple syrup for serving

In a large mixing bowl, whisk together flours, sugar, baking powder, salt, ginger, and cinnamon until they are well mixed. Add soymilk, oil, and vanilla and almond extracts. Use a hand blender to mix batter until smooth and lump-free.

Heat a griddle over medium-high heat and spray it with cooking spray. Pour out 1/4 cup batter per pancake. Cook pancakes until edges are firm and middle is bubbling. Flip and cook until both sides are golden brown. Serve pancakes topped with margarine and syrup.

Note: The batter can be stored in the refrigerator for several days.

Variations: For Blueberry Pancakes, add 2 cups frozen blueberries to pancake batter. For Cranberry-Pecan Pancakes, add 1 cup pecans and 1 cup dried cranberries to pancake batter. For Wheat Beer Pancakes, replace soymilk with a high-quality wheat beer for a unique and fluffy pancake.

Per serving (1/8 of recipe): 576 calories, 21.9 g fat, 3 g saturated fat, 33.4% calories from fat, 0 mg cholesterol • 10 g protein, 84.2 g carbohydrate, 33.9 g sugar, 3.8 g fiber • 781 mg sodium, 336 mg calcium, 4.5 mg iron, 0.4 mg vitamin C, 36 mcg beta-carotene, 7.6 mg vitamin E